# SIGNS *of* SALVATION
## New Life Where Grace and Truth Meet

*a biblical meditation*
*by*
**Ben Richmond**

*The law indeed was given through Moses;*
*grace and truth came through Jesus Christ.*
John 1:17, NRS

*The Lord . . . confirmed the message*
*by the signs that accompanied it.*
Mark 16:20, NRS

*Friends*
United Press
Richmond, Indiana

Library of Congress Cataloging-in-Publication Data

Richmond, Ben.
  Signs of salvation : new life where grace and truth meet : a biblical
meditation / by Ben Richmond.
    p. cm.
  Includes bibliographical references and index.
  ISBN-13: 978-0-944350-68-3 (pbk. : alk. paper)
  1. Salvation--Biblical teaching. 2. Sanctification. 3. Jesus
Christ--Ethics. 4. Christian life. 5. Conduct of life. 6. Christian life.
I. Title.
  BS680.S25R53 2005
  234--dc22

                    2005013906

# CONTENTS

Acknowledgments                                          v
Introduction: Fix Your Eyes Upon Jesus                   1
    A Living God                     2
    Thinking about Salvation         6

1  *Two Gardens and Two Trees*                 13
    The Garden of Eden and the New Jerusalem    13
    The Tree of Knowledge and the Tree of Life  24

2  *Salvation in this World and the Next*      35
    The Unconditional Covenant with Abraham      36
    The Covenant of Law with Moses   38
    The Everlasting Covenant with David   42
    The Covenant Broken              45
    The Day of Judgment              50

3  *The New Covenant*                          65
    'I will remember their sins no more.'   71
    'I will put my law within them.'   75
    'They will all know me.'          81
    Salvation in This World and the Next   86

**4** The Sign of the Listening Community 93
    The Mystery of Inclusion 98
    The Countersign of Mutual Submission 105
    The Throne of God and of the Lamb 117

**5** The Sign of the Bountiful Community 123
    The Mystery of Prosperity 123
    The Countersign of Jubilee 131
    The Marriage Feast of the Lamb 148

**6** The Sign of the Peaceable Community 155
    The Mystery of God as Warrior 157
    The Countersign of Immanuel 164
    The War of the Lamb 184

**7** The Sign of the Community of Grace and Truth 195
    The Mystery of Binding and Loosing 200
    The Countersign of Discipline 203
    Robes Washed in the Blood of the Lamb 211

**8** Baptism into New Life 215
    Baptism in Fire 218
    The Gift of New Life 227

Appendix 1: Discussion Questions 235
Appendix 2: Questions Concerning the Saved Life 239
Sources 245
Index of scripture citations 247

# ACKNOWLEDGMENTS

Special thanks to my wife, Jody Kerman Richmond, who fully participated in the development of the ideas in this book through endless discussions over many years, and to my mother, Evelyn Brown Richmond, for her editorial help and encouragement. As important was her life-long habit of faith seasoned with suspicion of too-easy answers. I dedicate this book to her.

Too many ministers, teachers, and writers to name have influenced my thinking. I have of course been shaped by the thought and experience of Friends, the church in which I have spent my adult life. T. Canby Jones, joyous minister of the Gospel among Friends and long-time professor of religion at Wilmington College, introduced me to the language of the Lamb's War. Many small groups helped me immeasurably by participating in studies of the first chapters of Genesis, which laid the foundation for Chapter 1. Thanks also to Jan Wood, Doug Gwyn, Patrick Nugent, Ann Miller, Wayne and Kay Carter, and Peggy Hollingsworth for their help along the way. I appreciate the vision of Winchester Friends Church and the financial support they provided through the Ed and Bashia Best fund.

[Ed. Note: Readers may contact the author at benrichmond@earthlink.net. ]

# INTRODUCTION:
# FIX YOUR EYES UPON JESUS

*S*alvation comes at the intersection of grace and truth, where God saves us from our enemies and all sorts of evil, not least of which is the evil within ourselves. It brings us into the joy and goodness that God intended from the beginning of creation and gives us hope for eternal life. This book is a rebellion against lesser ideas of salvation, particularly any that suggest people can be saved without the evidence of transformed lives. There is no salvation without signs of salvation.

This book had its genesis in a Winchell's Donut Shop in Portland, Oregon many years ago. A young man sat down, uninvited, at my table and asked if I was saved. He proceeded to take me through a pamphlet with cartoons that illustrated "the four spiritual laws." I learned that (1) God loves me and has a plan for my life, but (2) because of sin, there is a gulf between me and God, and (3) that Jesus died on the cross to bridge that chasm, and finally (4) that I needed to repent from my sins and ask Jesus into my heart as Lord and Savior. The pamphlet had a prayer that I could read and a statement that I could sign.

Even then, before I could articulate why, I sensed that this presentation fell woefully short of a genuinely biblical vision.

I do not fault it for being wrong so much as for being inadequate. I kept wondering, how can you talk about salvation and fail to reflect Jesus' passionate concern for peace and justice, and for the poor? Yet, my own attempts at political action felt legalistic and alienating. The young man's question, "Are you saved?" kept provoking me to look more deeply into the scripture and the cross.

This book is the fruit of that search. It presents a biblical understanding of salvation in which legalism is replaced with grace, and the cross is the entryway to a life transformed by Jesus' ethics.

Here is the plan. First, I briefly introduce myself and my methodology so you have some idea where I am coming from. The rest of the book is a meditation on the living voice of God. The first chapter offers a biblical vision of what the saved life looks like. The second chapter relates how the biblical understanding of salvation developed. That is the story of the convergence of four apparently contradictory imperatives: God's gift of unmerited love; God's demand for justice and purity; God's intervention to save people in this life; the hope for ultimate salvation in the next. These lines converge in Jesus' sacrifice on the cross, the subject of the third chapter. The remainder of the book explores the signs of salvation as they are lived out in the community of faith. It is a life of joy and power based on a listening relationship with our living God. At the end, I talk about baptism—not the ritual, but the costly experience of yielding to God that brings us into this life.

## A Living God

I grew up the only child of divorced parents. My father was an architect, highly analytical and an agnostic. My mother was a scholar of English literature and a Christian who, nevertheless, always carried some element of doubt with her faith. His rationalism and her question-filled faith shaped me. Then, as a young adult, over the course of a year, I had some extraordinary and transforming experiences of the presence of God.

I am not by nature prone to mystical experiences, and I am not of the opinion that seeing visions or hearing voices "proves" anything. These experiences certainly do not validate any truth claims I may make—though my claim to have had these experiences may prove something about me! I have been warned against making too much of these encounters. I should realize that these things were a sign of how very needy I was, not how worthy! In any event, the absolute certainty of Christ's living reality that these encounters provoked made me evangelical, but the intellectual inheritance from my parents made me skeptical of too easy piety. Here is what happened.

I was emotionally exhausted. My first wife had left me to escape my clinging neediness that psychologists might trace back to my childhood. The political activism for peace and justice that had given shape to my life from my high school years no longer felt compelling or clear. I was sitting with a few other men in quiet waiting influenced by Quaker worship: one considered himself a Buddhist, another an agnostic; I considered myself vaguely Christian. In that silence, for a moment—or was it longer?—I had a vision of eyes looking at me, enveloping me in totally unexpected love and compassion. I knew deeply, instinctively, that these were the eyes of Jesus and that he was looking at me from the cross.

That Jesus had chosen to come to me in compassion changed everything. Perhaps the immediate circumstances of my life continued, but my sense of reality was irrevocably altered. No longer was God a "concept," nor was Jesus an admirable but long-ago teacher of ethics. Here was the living God!

And, behold, God cared about me—even in the midst of my confusion and "untogetherness." In the pain and compassion of those eyes, I saw that at the center of the universe was love.

> Let us fix our eyes on Jesus, the author and perfecter of our faith, who for the joy set before him endured the cross, scorning its shame, and sat down at the right hand of the throne of God. (Hebrews 12:2, NIV)

Jesus is the "author" of faith because, in the end, faith is not based on deductions or principles of logic. Rational arguments for the existence of God that occupied the Scholastics are ultimately unsatisfying. Christian faith is the result of an encounter with a man who lived like us, and died, and yet lives. Christian faith is the response of hearts to the fact that Jesus has—in contradiction to all reason, and beyond any expectation—come to us in love.

This is grace: unreasonable, unearned, unanticipated, personal love, showered on us by the Living God. It is experienced in a thousand ways and conceived of in a hundred theories; it can never be fully comprehended, and its riches are inexhaustible.

Several months after Jesus changed forever my understanding of the universe, he came again to change my understanding of myself—this time as Light. I was, at the time, employed part-time as a dishwasher in a downtown restaurant. During the rush of a noon-time business lunch, surrounded by buckets piled high with dirty dishes, amid the clamor of servers needing clean plates, God chose to confront me again. I'll never know how the dishes got washed, but they did; perhaps it was symbolic of what was being done to my soul. At any rate, what happened was that I felt a light shining on me. It was no gentle glow, but a nearly blinding beam like the light of an interrogator in a police drama.

I later discovered that John the Apostle wrote about this aspect of God's Light. Generally we think of Jesus' claim to be the Light of the World as a comfort, but in John, after the famous verse about God loving the world so much that he sent his only begotten Son, we read:

> And this is the judgment, that the light has come into the world, and people loved darkness rather than light because their deeds were evil. For all who do evil hate the light and do not come to the light, so that their deeds may not be exposed. (John 3:19-20, NRSV)

Amid the din of dishwashing, I saw myself in the Light of Truth. Whereas I had, for instance, treasured an image of myself as a forbearing and forgiving Christian suffering patiently my former wife's infidelities, I now saw how emotionally manipulative I had been in relation to her. Where I had believed myself to be an advocate of peace, I saw the anger that alienated me from others. Where I had seen myself as a person of love and a promoter of life, I saw that—in the pursuit of my selfish aim of retaining my wife's affections—I had willed to get her pregnant even though I knew that the result would be abortion and thus the murder of my child. That pregnancy never happened but, in the Light, I now knew the truth of my heart: I was manipulative, selfish, a potential murderer, and totally self-deceived.

Even at the time that I was experiencing this vision, what struck me as peculiar was that I did not feel particularly shamed. Doubtless to the confusion of my friends, I began to announce, "I am a sinner." Surely not a badge of honor, it was for me a simple and even joyful reality: at the center of the universe was God's love, at its periphery my sin, and the gravitational force of love was greater than the entropy of sin. I now understood that it wasn't my loveableness that held the universe together, but God's. I didn't have to be my own Savior, much less the Savior of the world. Someone else had already done that!

In the prologue to the Gospel of John, comes a verse that appears on the title page:

> The law indeed was given through Moses, grace and truth came through Jesus Christ. (John 1:17, NRSV)

Is it not a defining mark of the divine, to be able to unite grace and truth? I am grateful that in my life Jesus has brought both, and that grace infused the truth when truth was difficult.

### Thinking about Salvation

Within a few months of my encounter with the Light, I heard within me the words, "Preach Christ." While the claim that God does indeed still speak is central to all that follows, this is the only time in my life that I can say I have "heard" the voice of God.

The message "preach Christ" was profoundly difficult for me. At that time in my life I distrusted preachers and didn't know much of Christ. But since the message was undeniable, I knew that the direction of my life was set. First I had to gain a language that would make preaching Christ even an intellectual possibility. Words like "grace," "sin," and "salvation," which have already appeared in this introduction, were not unknown to me—but they did not have any living content for me or for people in the circles in which I moved.

Even more of an obstacle was my impression, as an outsider to the evangelical church where I presumed such words were current, that salvation was thought of primarily in terms of personal "fire insurance." I was repulsed by a concept of salvation so individualistic and essentially selfish. Fear of a sulfur-belching hell had never been a motivator for me or my friends. Furthermore, in my experience, the churches that talked "salvation" seemed unconcerned with—if not hostile to—the great issues of peace, ecology, racism, equal rights, and economic justice. If their notion of salvation wasn't devoid of ethical content, it seemed to be narrowly restricted to sexual prohibitions. I'd seen surveys that claimed that the "born again" were ethically indistinguishable from their "unsaved" brothers and sisters. I had grown cynical about the reality of the salvation they proposed because it seemed so foreign to the character of the Jesus of whom I had read and of the life for which I yearned.

As I worked on the question of what it might mean to "preach Christ," I discovered something that must seem obvious: the term "Christianity" actively embraces a huge spectrum of ideas about even its most fundamental truths. Many ways of thinking about the atoning work of Christ have found wide acceptance in the history of the Christian church, and—this really surprised me—in its basic creedal affirmations, the church has made no effort to pin down the question of *how* Christ's death "saves." What wisdom! As if any formulation would be able to somehow "capture" the fullness of the breadth and depth of what Jesus accomplished in his life, ministry, death, and resurrection. And yet, I realized, *how* people conceive of salvation influences both the way they live and how they share their faith.

The range of thinking about the saving work of Christ has often been summarized in four theories of the atonement: the ransom theory, the satisfaction theory, the moral influence theory, and the substitutionary theory. Each enjoys a measure of biblical support. Each grows out of different understandings of just what "sin" is and how God works in human lives.

According to the ransom theory, Christ's death is the climax of a cosmic drama in which Christ overcomes the forces of evil. Satan has rights over humanity because of human sin and evil. The law of justice requires that God cannot overlook human evil—but out of love, God, in Christ, pays the penalty owed to Satan because of it. Satan, however, discovers he has, in a sense, been tricked: God's love is greater than the law of justice and, in the resurrection, life and love swallow up death and hatred. God takes Satan captive.

The satisfaction theory bears close relationship to theories of kingship that prevailed in the Middle Ages in Europe. The holy God's sovereign honor was so deeply offended by humanity's rebellion that it could never be satisfied by any human effort or sacrifice. Jesus Christ, the sinless Son of God, offered himself as the pure sacrifice, satisfying God's offended honor. This opened the channel for the communication of God's grace through the sacraments and for the operation of the Holy Spirit in the lives of sinful men and women.

Often contrasted with the satisfaction theory, the moral influence theory of the atonement emphasizes that Christ is the great Teacher. Above all, by the sacrificial and selfless love he displayed on the cross, Christ arouses a responsive love in people of faith. It is this love on which our reconciliation and forgiveness rest. The cross reveals how humanity rejects God's love, but also how God graciously overcomes that rejection. When we allow that example to penetrate our hearts, our relationship to God is transformed, and we have been saved.

The substitutionary theory of the atonement has been the dominant formulation, particularly among evangelicals since the Reformation. A recent formulation of it says in part:

> God "justifies the wicked" . . . by imputing . . . righteousness to them and ceasing to count their sins against them (Rom. 4:1-8). Sinners receive through faith in Christ alone "the gift of righteousness" (Rom. 1:17; 5:1; Phil. 3:9) and thus become "the righteousness of God" in him who was "made sin" for them (2 Cor. 5:21).
>
> As our sins were reckoned to Christ, so Christ's righteousness is reckoned to us. This is justification by the imputation of Christ's righteousness. All we bring to the transaction is our need of it. . . .[1]

This is the theory behind "the four spiritual laws." Because Jesus substitutes his life for ours, when God looks at us he sees only the purity of Jesus. Jesus pays the penalty for our sin on the cross.

Each of these theories has its strengths and weaknesses. The ransom theory glories in God's sovereign power in the cosmic conflict between good and evil but can seem distantly removed from human experience. The moral influence theory, its flip side, perceives Jesus as simply another great teacher, reducing salvation to human effort. In contrast, the satisfaction theory emphasizes the majesty and grace of God toward society as a mass, as the substitutionary theory does toward the believer as an individual, but these two theories, each in its own way, tend to sever the atoning work of Christ from ethical transformation and thus to undercut God's demand of holiness.

In this book, I reflect on atonement through the lens of the new covenant promise that was first articulated by the prophet

Jeremiah. My purpose is to find a way to describe salvation that is more adequate to the whole biblical vision: the atoning work of Jesus on the cross not only presents us as acceptable before God by God's declaration (justification), but actually changes believers from the *inside* so that they begin to have in actuality the righteousness that God requires (sanctification). In using this approach, I am guided by the joyful cry of evangelicalism, "by grace alone, through faith alone, because of Christ alone." Biblical salvation is based in grace *and* truth, thus fulfilling the law of God.

I have found it helpful to concentrate on how the Bible uses the terminology of salvation and to couch what I have to say solely in biblical imagery and biblical language. In all that follows, my text is littered with passages of scripture. This does not mean that I (or anyone else) can avoid interpretation when it comes to reading scripture or selecting which passages to quote, so it is only fair to tell what principles I have used.

The first principle is that the canon of scripture, and the text of scriptures as we have them now, are inspired by God and are authoritative in matters of faith. Historical and critical studies help us know how to read the texts but do not give us a basis for choosing some texts as more authoritative or inspired than others (nor for resorting to presumed earlier or more "authentic" constructions). A second principle is my belief that the texts should be read for what the words say; if a text is silent on a question that interests us, we have to be content with the silence. It is important to distinguish when the scriptures are describing human actions and thoughts as opposed to when they are attributing thoughts and actions to God. Finally, the great thing is to "fix our eyes on Jesus, the author and perfecter of our faith." Jesus Christ is the interpretive key, and in him the law and the prophets have their fulfillment.

While I would never claim to be a student of Karl Barth, into whose great *Church Dogmatics* I have only dipped, I aspire to approach scripture with his appreciation for the primacy of the word of God in contrast to the demythologizing school of his contemporary, Rudolf Bultmann. There is a story that, once, during a lecture on the Book of Genesis, a student challenged Barth with the question, "Do you yourself really believe that the serpent spoke in the Garden of Eden?" Barth replied, "In the end, whether the serpent spoke or not is not important; what is important is what he said!" I hope to emulate the intentional naiveté of that response.

Any truly adequate understanding of the saving work of God must acknowledge that salvation wrenches believers out of the alienation and isolation of their individual lives and thrusts them into the great historic company of the *people* whom God is blessing and forming to be a blessing to others. Salvation is for individuals, but it is also a community enterprise. Salvation is the root of personal righteousness, but it is also the root of the social justice and peace for which the earth longs.

I hope this book will be helpful to individuals and will also provoke the formation of small groups to "walk in the Light" together—opening up the inner places of their lives before God and one another. To that end, I have attached two appendices with materials that can be used by groups to carry on exploration of the ideas found in the main text. The first provides discussion questions for each chapter. The second takes questions developed in my faith tradition—the Friends church (also known as Quakers)—as a basis for what we call "worship sharing." I am confident that not only will piety and love of God deepen, but holy boldness will enable believers to seek together to shake off the personal and cultural "sin that so easily entangles."

It is all a gift from God. Love, life itself, and hope for a new heaven and a new earth; none of this is our doing—it is all grace. In the end, the thesis of this book is that the community of those who are gathered together in this faith can become the sign of God's saving power, now and into eternity.

> I pray that, according to the riches of his glory, he may grant that *you may be strengthened in your inner being* with power through his Spirit, and that Christ may dwell in your hearts through faith, as you are being rooted and grounded in love. I pray that you may have the power to comprehend, with all the saints, what is the breadth and length and height and depth, and to know the love of Christ that surpasses knowledge, so that you may be filled with all the fullness of God.
>
> Now to him who by the power at work within us is able to accomplish abundantly far more than all we can ask or imagine, to him be *glory in the church* and in Christ Jesus to all generations, forever and ever. Amen. (Ephesians 3:16-21, NRSV, my emphasis)

---

[1] "The Gospel of Jesus Christ: An Evangelical Celebration," in R. C. Sproul, *Getting the Gospel Right: The Tie That Binds Evangelicals Together*, Baker Books, 1999, Appendix 2.

# TWO GARDENS AND TWO TREES

*S*alvation history begins in Genisis with the story of the creation and the expulsion of Adam and Eve from the Garden of Eden. It ends in Revelation with the creation of the new heavens and new earth. These two stories, separated vastly in the time of their writing and even more vastly in the times of which they speak, have at their heart the picture of two gardens.[1] Or, it would be more accurate to say, one garden is pictured twice. The two gardens do not look alike: one, at the beginning of creation, is completely pastoral—rich in natural resources, abounding in animal life and populated only by one couple; the other, at the close of the era, is located within a city's walls, and teems with hundreds of thousands of men and women. But we know it is the same garden because at the center of both is a river, and with the river a tree: the tree of life. When we look at life in the garden, we see how radical a picture God has painted of the saved life.

## *The Garden of Eden and the New Jerusalem*

This garden is paradise,[2] a word that, scripturally speaking, first appears in Genesis:

> And the Lord God planted a garden/*paradeison* in Eden (Genesis 2:8, NRSV)

and is last found in Revelation:

> To everyone who conquers, I will give permission
> to eat from the tree of life that is in the paradise/
> *paradeiso* of God. (Revelation 2:7b, NRSV)

To live in this garden and eat of the tree of life, may then be
said to be the goal of salvation.

"Heaven" as the goal of salvation is often conceived of in
abstract, other-worldly terms. But this is not biblical. The biblical writers refuse to sever the spirit from the body. So (when
adopting a biblical view) it is better to imagine salvation in
terms of return to the garden/*paradeison* after years of exile,
than it is to imagine it as a disembodied afterlife of the spirit-
world. In the scriptures, salvation, even when considered solely
in terms of the afterlife, is *life*: the life of the bodily resurrection.

The early church celebrated salvation in rich and earthy
terms. Here is a hymn about the experience of salvation that
was sung by Christians in the first centuries:

> My heart was pruned and its flower appeared,
> then grace sprang up in it,
> and it produced fruits for the Lord.
>
> For the Most High circumcised me by his Holy
>   Spirit,
> then he uncovered my inward being toward him,
> and filled me with his love.
>
> And his circumcising became my salvation,
> and I ran in the Way in his peace,
> in the Way of truth.
> . . . . . . . . . . . . . . . . . .
> And he took me to his Paradise,
> wherein is the wealth of the Lord's pleasure.

((I contemplated blooming and fruit-bearing trees,
and self-grown was their crown.

Their branches were flourishing and their fruits
   were shining;
their roots (were) from an immortal land.

And a river of gladness was irrigating them,
and the region round about them is the land of
   eternal life.))

Then I adored the Lord because of his
   magnificence.

And I said, blessed, O Lord, are they
who are planted in your land,
and who have a place in your Paradise;

And who grow in the growth of your trees
and have passed from darkness into light.
. . . . . . . . . . . . . . . . . . . . . . . . . . . . . . . . . . . .
Indeed, there is much room in your Paradise.

And there is nothing in it which is barren,
but everything is filled with fruit.
Praise be to you, O God, the delight of Paradise
   for ever.

Hallelujah.[3]

Blessed, indeed, are those who are planted in the garden of the
Lord. What will it be like?[4]

The first eleven chapters of Genesis comprise the story of
beginnings: the wisdom of God in creation, and an account of
how we have come to experience a life so at odds with that wisdom. Here is the first place to look if we would like to know
what the paradisal life feels and tastes like.

15

There are two creation narratives at the beginning. The first is the majestic account of the seven days of creation (Genesis 1–2:4a). Then follows the story of humanity in the garden/ *paradeison* (Genesis 2:4b through 3:6), which is contrasted sharply with the account of life "outside" (Genesis 3:7 through Chapter 11). The dividing point is the account of Adam and Eve eating the forbidden fruit, which results in their removal from the Garden. By comparing features of life as God intended it before that act and as we experience it afterwards, we get a compelling impression of the consequence of "the fall" and a picture of the original hope God had—and still has—for us.

Here we arrive at the heart of the Good News, for as we examine life in paradise, we see signposts to what the saved life might look like. The overarching structure of the Bible (from Adam and Eve's first enjoyment of the Garden in Genesis to our return to the Garden in the Book of Revelation) indicates that God's goal is to save humanity from the consequence of Adam and Eve's rebellion and restore us to the life God intended for us from the creation.

*the sign of creativity*

The first striking thing that emerges from the scriptural text is the relationship between humanity/*adam* and the ground/*adamah*: "the Lord God formed *adam* from the dust of *adamah*" (Genesis 2:7, NRSV). Humanity is rooted in a sense of home; even the Hebrew words say, "this is where we belong." Placed in the garden that is watered by the river that flowed from Eden, humankind was charged with important work: "The Lord God took *adam* and put him in the garden of Eden to till it and keep it" (Genesis 2:15, NRSV). The church has often said that humanity's task is to "love God and glorify him forever," but the scripture has a more practical job description: the nurture of God's creation.

Then God formed every animal, and brought them all to *adam* "to see what he would call them" (Genesis 2:19, NRSV). Naming things creates order out of chaos. *Adam's* naming of the animals reflects the great naming God did in creation, when

> the earth was a formless void and darkness covered the face of the deep, while a wind from God swept over the face of the waters. (Genesis 1:2, NRSV)

God started to speak and named "light, and it was light" and then named light, "Day," and darkness, "Night," and so with water and all the things and beings of creation. Similarly, in paradise, people are entrusted with the responsibility to create order out of chaos, to care for the creation, and to nurture its fruitfulness.

But people experience the earth and work very differently:

> ". . . cursed is the ground because of you; in toil you shall eat of it all the days of your life; thorns and thistles it shall bring forth for you; and you shall eat the plants of the field. By the sweat of your face you shall eat bread until you return to the ground. . . . " (Genesis 3:17b-19a, NRSV)

Some people have an idea of heaven as boring or meaningless—so that it has no allure, and "salvation" seems irrelevant. But boring and meaningless toil are signs of the curse that results from humanity's rebellion against God. A sign of salvation is the experience of work as meaningful and creative. In salvation, we are co-laborers-with-God in caring for and giving meaningful order to the creation.

*the sign of abundance*

As soon as God put humanity/*adam* in the garden/*paradeison*, God brought out of the ground/*adamah* "every tree that is pleasant to the sight and good for food" (Genesis 2:9, NRSV). There was a four-branched river (recall the semi-arid conditions of Palestine to understand the wealth that represents); there was gold, bdelium[5] and onyx. Almost by way of a parenthesis the account adds, "the gold of that land is good" (Genesis 2:12, NRSV). Abundant water, abundant fruit, abundant wealth is a promised land, indeed!

Contrast this with the "thorns and thistles" the ground brings forth in response to the unrelenting toil of humanity after the rebellion, and you have the picture. A sign of salvation is relief from the fear of scarcity through enjoyment of the abundance of Eden. In salvation, we are free of fear because we know we have enough.

*the sign of peace*

After Adam and Eve have been expelled from the garden and have established a family, the first social interaction reported is the murder of one of their children by the other. And the murder of Abel by Cain is only the beginning! Violence tears apart the social fabric of human society after the rebellion. By the end of the same chapter, Lamech, the fifth generation in descent from Cain, boasts to his two wives:

> "Adah and Zillah, hear my voice; you wives of Lamech, listen to what I say: I have killed a man for wounding me, a young man for striking me. If Cain is avenged sevenfold, truly Lamech seventy-sevenfold." (Genesis 4:23b-24, NRSV)

In just three more generations comes Noah and the flood. Events have been moving along quickly, but nothing has moved along as quickly as the multiplication of violence.

> The Nephilim were on the earth in those days—and also afterward—when the sons of God went in to the daughters of humans/*adam*, who bore children to them.[6] These were the heroes that were of old, warriors of renown. The Lord saw that the wickedness of humankind was great in the earth, and that every inclination of the thoughts of their hearts was only evil continually. . . .
>
> Now the earth was corrupt in God's sight, and the earth was filled with violence.[7] And God saw that the earth was corrupt; for all flesh had corrupted its ways upon the earth. And God said to Noah, "I have determined to make an end of all flesh, for the earth is filled with violence because of them; now I am going to destroy them along with the earth." (Genesis 6:4-5, 11-13, NRSV)

The whole earth was so corrupted by violence that, looking at it, God was grieved and "repented" of making humanity/*adam* (Genesis 6:6, KJV).

But recall, the earth had been made "good," and Eden was a pleasure-park of harmony and peace. A sign of salvation is the restoration of the peace that flourished in paradise. In salvation, we dwell in peace regardless of the turmoil that may swirl around us.

*the signs of community and equality*

The story of Eden begins after the first account of creation, which is marked by the seven-fold affirmation, "And God saw that it was good." It is in the Garden that God, for the first

SIGNS *of* SALVATION

time, declares something to be "not good." Perhaps surprisingly, it is not said of the serpent who tempts Eve to eat from the forbidden fruit. Rather, the first evil is the loneliness of the solitary person:

> Then the Lord God said, "It is not good that *adam* should be alone; I will make him a helper as his partner." (Genesis 2:18, NRSV)

So God created all the animals, but none would serve as suitable "help meet" for *adam* (Genesis 2:20, KJV). Then, as humanity/*adam* had been formed out of the ground/*adamah*, so a woman/*ishah* was formed out of man/*ish*. This is the first use of the gender-specific terms "man" and "woman" in the Bible; heretofore, humanity in general (that is *adam*) was under discussion. So, woman and man were created to be helpers and partners, one for another. This was the means God used to overcome the first evil, loneliness.

By the way, it is important to note that there is no hint of subordination in the word "helpmeet." Indeed, the term was frequently used as an attribute of God; for instance in Jacob's blessing, "by the God of your father, who will help you" (Genesis 49:25, NRSV); and, "But surely, God is my helper; the Lord is the upholder of my life" (Psalm 54:4, NRSV). Until the rebellion, this equality of being helpers characterized the relationship between man and woman. But after the rebellion, Eve heard this curse:

> To the woman he said, "I will greatly increase your pangs in childbearing; in pain you shall bring forth children, yet your desire shall be for your husband, *and he shall rule over you.*" (Genesis 3:16, NRSV, my emphasis)

*20*

Thus patriarchy (the rule of males over females) is a result of the rebellion. A sign of salvation is community life in which all people are honored as mutual help-mates, one of the other. In salvation, we are free from loneliness, and this can only be realized where we are free to be together with one another as equals.

### the sign of unashamed sexuality

One of the joyful aspects of the Hebrew scripture is its view of sexuality. It is unaffected in its appreciation of sexual pleasure:

> Let your fountain be blessed, and rejoice in the wife of your youth, a lovely deer, a graceful doe. May her breasts satisfy you at all times; may you be intoxicated always by her love." (Proverbs 5:18-19, NRSV)

And, of course, from the Song of Solomon in which the female voice is heard as well as the male:

> O that you were like a brother to me,
>     who nursed at my mother's breast!
> If I met you outside, I would kiss you,
>     and no one would despise me.
> I would lead you and bring you into the house
>         of my mother,
>     and into the chamber of the one who bore me.
> I would give you spiced wine to drink,
>     the juice of my pomegranates.
> O that his left hand were under my head,
>     and that his right hand embraced me!
>                     (Song of Solomon 8:1-3, NRSV)

The scripture shows awareness of the deep significance of sexual intimacy:

> ... a man leaves his father and his mother and clings
> to his wife, and they become one flesh. (Genesis
> 2:24, NRSV)

Here a family—the basic structure of society—is formed,
and it is based on something new and inviolable: the becoming
"one flesh" of man and woman. Where before there were two,
there is now one. The phrase "one flesh" implies an emotional
and spiritual, as well as physical, union charged with the potential and awesome significance of creating new life.

Before the rebellion, Adam and Eve were "naked, and were
not ashamed" (Genesis 2:25, NRSV). It was only in the rebellion that they knew shame in their nakedness.

> They heard the sound of the Lord God walking in
> the garden at the time of the evening breeze, and the
> man and his wife hid themselves from the presence
> of the Lord God among the trees of the garden.
>
> But the Lord God called to the man, and said to him,
> "Where are you?"
>
> He said, "I heard the sound of you in the garden, and
> I was afraid, because I was naked; and I hid myself."
> (Genesis 3:8-10, NRSV)

A sign of salvation is the quality of relationship between
male and female conducted so that there is no shame in the
sexual experience, but awe at the power it holds to transform
two individuals into "one flesh." In salvation, we rejoice in
knowing ourselves both sexual and good in the eyes of God.

*the sign of integrity*

When it was said of Adam and Eve that they were "naked,
and were not ashamed," not only physical nakedness but also

openness of heart and soul were implied.[8] The relationship between Adam and Eve changed when they ate of the forbidden fruit. Immediately, they started to prevaricate and cast blame. The dialogue would be humorous, were it not so tragic:

> [God] said, "Who told you that you were naked? Have you eaten from the tree of which I commanded you not to eat?"
>
> The man said, "The woman whom you gave to be with me, she gave me fruit from the tree, and I ate."
>
> Then the Lord God said to the woman, "What is this that you have done?"
>
> The woman said, "The serpent tricked me, and I ate." (Genesis 3:11-13, NRSV)

Contrast this sorry passing of responsibility with the integrity of the woman's answer to the "wily serpent" before the rebellion:

> Now the serpent was more crafty than any other wild animal that the Lord God had made. He said to the woman, "Did God say, 'You shall not eat from any tree in the garden'?"
>
> The woman said to the serpent, "We may eat of the fruit of the trees in the garden; but God said, 'You shall not eat of the fruit of the tree that is in the middle of the garden, nor shall you touch it, or you shall die.'" (Genesis 3:1-3, NRSV)

A sign of salvation is the internal ability to maintain openness and transparency in one's life, which results in integrity in one's dealings and in truth-speaking. In salvation, we know the truth about ourselves in the assurance of complete love; we can afford to be honest.

The story of Eden has more riches to unfold, but at a minimum, we can see that in the wisdom of Creation, God intended for us a life—a paradisal life—characterized by creativity, abundance, peace, community, equality, wholesome sexuality, and integrity. This kind of life is the fruit of salvation.

But, what are its roots? To answer that question, we must seek to understand why God forbade humanity to eat of the tree of the knowledge of good and evil and yet put into the Garden a serpent to tempt them to do just that.

### The Tree of Knowledge and the Tree of Life

There were all sorts of trees in Eden, but only two are named:

> Out of the ground the Lord God made to grow every tree that is pleasant to the sight and good for food, the tree of life also in the midst of the garden, and the tree of the knowledge of good and evil. (Genesis 2:9, NRSV)

Humanity had free use of all these trees—but one.

> And the Lord God commanded the man, "You may freely eat of every tree of the garden; but of the tree of the knowledge of good and evil you shall not eat, for in the day that you eat of it you shall die." (Genesis 2:16-17, NRSV)

In Eden only one tree was barred, and God explains that to eat of it brings death. Indeed, one looks in vain to find the tree of the knowledge of good and evil in the New Jerusalem, for "nothing accursed will be found there any more" (Revelation

22:3a, NRSV). Why does God say that this particular tree brings death?

First, it is crucially important to notice that the tree is not simply the "tree of knowledge." It is, rather, the tree of a certain kind of knowledge: "the knowledge of good and evil." Scientific knowledge, or the kind of knowing that allows Adam and Eve to carry out their tasks of "naming," "tilling," and "nurturing" is not what God has barred. The knowledge of good and evil is, in its essence, the capacity to decide what is "good" and therefore ought to be, and what is "evil" and therefore ought not to be.

In the creation, God exercised this capacity:

> In the beginning when God created the heavens and the earth, the earth was a formless void and darkness covered the face of the deep, while a wind from God swept over the face of the waters.
>
> Then God said, "Let there be light"; and there was light. And God saw that the light was good; and God separated the light from the darkness. (Genesis 1:1-4, NRSV)

God spoke forth light and sky, water and earth, vegetation, sun and moon, all the living creatures of sky, water and earth, and, finally humankind. At every step, God looked and declared, "it was good." It is upon that divine knowledge of goodness that permission for existence rests. When God saw humankind's loneliness, God knew that it was "not good" and God obliterated this "not good" through the distinction of male and female companionship. The knowledge of what is good and what is evil is the essence of the Creator's right to judge the creation, to bless or destroy it. All moral judgment, human or divine, partakes—in degree—of this quality of blessing or destruction.

God understood that the knowing of good and evil was a power too great to be held by a creature—even by so marvelous a creature as *adam*. If humanity took on the role of judgment regarding good and evil, they would become (as the serpent had truly said they would) god-like and, thus, rival gods to the One God. The exercise of that power would inevitably bring destruction upon the one who wielded it, and upon the creation as well. In mercy to humanity, God made a clear prohibition against this kind of "knowing."

Only God can finally know reality comprehensively enough to make right judgments regarding good and evil: the undeniable reality of the human condition is that we know things only in part, only subjectively. All of our knowing is shaped by culture, ideology, and the limitations of our particular circumstances.

It is for these reasons that it is not permissible to eat from both the tree of the knowledge of good and evil and the tree of life.

> Then the Lord God said, "See, the man has become like one of us, knowing good and evil; and now, he might reach out his hand and take also from the tree of life, and eat, and live forever." (Genesis 3:22, NRSV)

The jealousy of God (unlike many human jealousies) is based in the knowledge that rivalry with God in this matter of judging good and evil inevitably leads to chaos and the destruction of the good. The spread of violence chronicled in Genesis 4-11 is evidence of the real-life evil that follows the human arrogation of the divine power to judge. The prohibition against eating the fruit of the tree of the knowledge of good and evil simultaneously with the permission to eat of the tree of life was God's gracious provision to save humanity and the rest of creation from the awful fate of uniting demonic destructiveness with everlasting life. The expulsion from Eden, which seems so harsh, is in fact the expression of God's gracious protection of the creation.

The question remains, if the tree of knowledge of good and evil was so destructive, why was it there in Eden at all? There would be no answer to this if the tree were, in fact, merely the tree of death, and the prohibition against eating its fruit merely an arbitrary test placed over humanity by a distrustful God.

The tree of knowledge of good and evil, as long as it remains uneaten, stands as the witness of humanity's willing acknowledgment of God's sovereignty as the judge of good and evil.[9] The presence of the tree signifies humanity's freedom to accept—or reject—this distinction between Creator and created. The presence of the tree, and the serpent who points to it, stand for God's radical offer of freedom—the freedom even to reject God.

Scripture is clear in pinning the corruption of the "heart" (which is where the Bible locates the will) on the universal human tendency to usurp moral judgment from God. This is what Eve and Adam chose to do. It is the original sin. The Eden story is reenacted in each individual as he or she makes the choice to rebelliously assert moral independence from God. Our individual guilt, condemnation, and death arise precisely from our freely chosen reenactment[10] of Adam's and Eve's rebellion. The alternative was—and is—to live in dependence upon God's prerogative to speak forth the judgment of good and evil.

*the tree of life*

In the paradise of Eden it was permissible to eat the fruit of the tree of life so long as the fruit of the knowledge of good and evil was rejected. The tree of life appears again in the garden of the New Jerusalem. Here is John's vision of the New Jerusalem:

> Then the angel showed me the river of the water of life, bright as crystal, flowing from the throne of God and of the Lamb through the middle of the street of the city. On either side of the river is the tree of life with its twelve kinds of fruit, producing its fruit each month; and the leaves of the tree are for the healing of the nations. (Revelation 22:1-2, NRSV)

John's phrase about "healing of the nations" suggests that the tree of life brings healing from the wounds of our rebellion so that we can enjoy the quality of life signaled in the description of Eden.

In the New Jerusalem, where the tree of the knowledge of good and evil is no more, sits the throne of God and the Lamb,

> "And the city has no need of sun or moon to shine on it, for the glory of God is its light, and its lamp is the Lamb. The nations will walk by its light . . . (Revelation 21:23-24a, NRSV)

To walk by the light of the Lamb of God is to live in obedience to his guidance. As life itself bursts forth from the word and breath of God, so the tree of life[11], standing on the banks of the river of God, is the wellspring of life, and we are invited to feast of it. The tree stands symbolically for the experience of eternal life.

28

Eternal life in this picture is neither static nor individualistic. Again:

> the tree of life with its twelve kinds of fruit, producing its fruit each month; and the leaves of the tree are for the healing of the nations. (Revelation 22:2, NRSV)

Its fruit varies by the season; it overshadows the nations and brings healing and peace. According to John's vision, we have come to the place where we can hear the voice of God (and we know it is God, indeed, for it is the voice of creation):

> And I heard a loud voice from the throne saying, "See, the home of God is among mortals. He will dwell with them; they will be his peoples, and God himself will be with them; he will wipe every tear from their eyes. Death will be no more; mourning and crying and pain will be no more, for the first things have passed away." And the one who was seated on the throne said, "See, I am making all things new." Also he said, "Write this, for these words are trustworthy and true." Then he said to me, "It is done! I am the Alpha and the Omega, the beginning and the end. To the thirsty I will give water as a gift from the spring of the water of life." (Revelation 21:3-6, NRSV)

The place of the tree of life, of the water of life, is the place where the voice of the creator God is heard. This was the essence of Eden as well. Recall the passage about how Adam and Eve conversed with God:

> They heard the sound of the Lord God walking in the garden at the time of the evening breeze. (Genesis 3:8a, NRSV)

The King James Version, in a more literal translation of the Hebrew, reads, "They heard *the voice of the Lord God walking* . . . ." [my emphasis] The *qol Yahweh*/the voice of the Lord, moved in the Garden at the time of the evening "breeze," which is a translation of the Hebrew, *ruach*, wind or spirit. The text points to the hope that we may hear the voice of God among us at the time of the Spirit's moving.[13]

It is the *qol Yahweh* who properly determines "good" and "evil." It is our failure to attend to the *qol Yahweh* that brings destruction and death. The story of Cain and Abel underscores this point.

> In the course of time Cain brought to the Lord an offering of the fruit of the ground, and Abel for his part brought of the firstlings of his flock, their fat portions. And the Lord had regard for Abel and his offering, but for Cain and his offering he had no regard. So Cain was very angry, and his countenance fell.
>
> The Lord said to Cain, "Why are you angry, and why has your countenance fallen? If you do well, will you not be accepted? And if you do not do well, sin is lurking at the door; its desire is for you, but you must master it."
>
> Cain said to his brother Abel, "Let us go out to the field." And when they were in the field, Cain rose up against his brother Abel, and killed him. (Genesis 4:3-8, NRSV)

Cain brought an offering to God, as did Abel. God accepts Abel's, but not Cain's. The text offers no explanation. It is tempting to speculate about what was wrong with Cain's offering, but that misses the point of the text. Silence about the ground of God's judgment is the point: the sin that was lurking at Cain's door, was his desire to judge his offering "good." God's judgment was that it was not. God's reasoning is not the issue; it is God's right to judge good and evil. To "do well" in Cain's case—as in all cases!—would be to accept the judgment of God about what was good and what was not good.

*the flaming sword and the lake of fire*

When human beings expropriated God's role as judge of good and evil, setting themselves up as rival gods, God responded by exiling them from the garden, cutting them off from access to the tree of life and setting a barrier to guard the way back to it:

> He drove out *adam*; and at the east of the garden of Eden he placed the cherubim, and a sword flaming and turning to guard the way to the tree of life. (Genesis 3:24, NRSV)

The way back to the tree of life goes through fire. The flaming sword that guards the way into the Garden of Eden has its parallel in the Book of Revelation in the lake of fire that appears before the New Jerusalem in which we again find the tree of life. This is how John the Revelator saw it:

> Then Death and Hades were thrown into the lake of fire. This is the second death, the lake of fire; and anyone whose name was not found written in the book of life was thrown into the lake of fire.

> Then I saw a new heaven and a new earth; for the first heaven and the first earth had passed away, and the sea was no more. (Revelation 20:14-15, 21:1, NRSV)

The vision of eternal life given to John was gloriously open-hearted and expansive. Myriads upon myriads stream through the twelve gates of the city and receive their welcome.

> Its gates will never be shut by day—and there will be no night there. People will bring into it the glory and the honor of the nations. But nothing unclean will enter it, nor anyone who practices abomination or falsehood, but only those who are written in the Lamb's book of life. (Revelation 21:25-27, NRSV)

The fire of the lake, and the fire of the various vials of God's wrath that preceded it have burnt up all that was evil and impure. The lake of fire outside the New Jerusalem, like the flaming sword, stands for the mighty purifying power of God to cleanse away all that is wicked and corrupt. Nothing impure can stand against the flaming sword that God has set to guard the way to the tree of life.

In Paradise, in the new heavens and new earth, God gets once more to sit as Judge. God gets to decide what is good and evil. Evil is obliterated. This story of the two Gardens and the two Trees is the framework within which the history of salvation is played out. It gives us a vision of the goodness that God intended from the beginning, and the ultimate expectation of that goodness restored. Salvation depends on our willingness to attend to the living voice of God. The biblical narrative shows how difficult this is.

[1] Literary criticism of the scripture demonstrates many strands of oral and written tradition and the hands of many "redactors." Nevertheless, I am treating the Hebrew and Christian scripture as a whole, because an overall unity of composition is discernible in this apparent literary jumble that seems to me to be evidence of a Hand beyond the human hands at work.

[2] The word "paradise" derives from Ecclesiastical Latin, *paradisus*, "heaven," "abode of the blessed," which in turn derives from Latin, "park," "orchard," borrowed directly from the Greek *paradeisos*, "park," "garden," or "pleasure-grounds."

[3] Ode 11, "The Odes of Solomon" in *The Old Testament Pseudepigrapha*, James Charlesworth, ed., Vol. 2, (Garden City, NY: Doubleday & Company, Inc., 1985) 744-746. Charlesworth says, "the Odes are a window through which we can occasionally glimpse the earliest Christians at worship . . ." (Vol. 2:728)

[4] By posing this question, I do not mean to assert a specific historical time or geographical place for either Eden or the New Jerusalem. The scriptures are not so much concerned with events in time as they are concerned with their meaning: i.e., "etiology" (the reason why things are as they are), and "eschatology" (the exploration of the ultimate resolution of things, how things will be).

[5] Bdelium may have been an aromatic gum; it appears only here and in Numbers 11:7. In the Septuagint it is translated here as *anthrax*, i.e., coal, and in Numbers, as *krystallos*, i.e., crystal.

[6] The passage about the sexual relations between the "sons of god" and "the daughters of men" has puzzled many a commentator. It seems to me that historical criticism correctly shows it to reflect a critique of a Canaanite orgiastic cult. For the text, however, the significance of this clearly illegitimate alliance is that its offspring, the Nephilim, are characterized as "warriors of renown" and thus as further evidence of the infiltration of violence into society. Their only other appearance is in Numbers 13:33 where the Israelite spies who had explored the promised land reported back that, "we seemed like grasshoppers" in relationship to them.

⁷ The word for violence, *hamas*, refers to human violence against the social order. A false witness is *hamas* (Deuteronomy 19:16) Simeon and Levi, who killed men in anger and for a whim hamstrung oxen, are said to have *hamas* in their swords (Genesis 49:5).

⁸ Cf., Job 26:6 "Sheol is naked before God, and Abaddon has no covering" (NRSV).

⁹ See Karl Barth, *Church Dogmatics*, III, Creation I, New York, Scribner, 1955-1963, pages 257-261 for a discussion of the two trees, which I found particularly helpful.

¹⁰ The scriptures do not impute guilt to a child prior to "the time he knows how to refuse the evil and choose the good" (Isaiah 7:15, NRSV). When Paul (loosely quoting from the opening verses of Psalms 14 and 53) writes

. . . all, both Jews and Greeks, are under the power of sin, as it is written: "There is no one who is righteous, not even one; there is no one who has understanding, there is no one who seeks God. All have turned aside, together they have become worthless; there is no one who shows kindness, there is not even one." (Romans 3:9b-12, NRSV)

Here Paul recognizes that the free decision to "turn aside" is the basis of guilt. In this, God is just, not imputing guilt where guilt has not been earned.

¹¹ Wisdom, in Proverbs 3:13-20, is "a tree of life to those who lay hold of her" (NRSV). According to Paul, "Christ Jesus . . . became for us wisdom from God, and righteousness and sanctification and redemption" (1 Corinthians 1:30, NRSV). Compare also the vision in Ezekiel of the river flowing from the Temple of God, on the banks of which are trees whose leaves are for healing (Ezekiel 47:1-12).

¹² That Yahweh is a living God who speaks distinguishes the God of Israel from all other gods and philosophies. Of idols, the prophets say:

If one cries out to it, it does not answer or save anyone from trouble. (Isaiah 46:7b, NRSV)

# SALVATION IN THIS WORLD AND THE NEXT

*J*n popular religion there is a tendency to use the term "salvation" to refer exclusively to the assurance of heaven (and avoidance of hell) after this life. That does not reflect the terminology of salvation in the Bible. Most references to God's saving work concern the many ways God intervenes in this life to physically rescue men and women from the dangers they face.[1] In the Hebrew Bible, the defining experience of salvation was the Exodus—God's intervention to save the Hebrew people from slavery in Egypt. As the biblical story continued, the Israelites saw God's saving hand in their economic and physical well-being, in deliverance from surrounding enemies, and in the establishment of Israel as a political entity that was understood to be the kingdom of God.

Later, when the Kingdom of Israel fell before the Babylonian and Persian empires, the people of God came to understand that salvation could no longer be defined by a political kingdom. God saved a special remnant. Under the pressure of continuing extreme oppression, a new hope for salvation began to be articulated by the prophets: God would create a new heaven and earth, radically bringing to an end the evil that seems so overpowering in this world. The people of God began to understand that salvation includes the hope for safe passage into the life of the resurrection where the righteous will enjoy a creation newly remade.

In the Bible, then, the concept of salvation unfolded in step with the history of God's relationship with the people of God. New and broader understandings of God's saving work expanded the earlier concept of salvation.

It is useful to trace the unfolding understanding of salvation by looking at the various covenants God established with the Hebrew people over time. Through these covenants two lines of tension eventually converge in the Christian understanding of salvation. The first line of tension is between *unconditional grace* and God's *requirement of righteousness and justice*. The second is between God's saving work *in this world* and with the hope for salvation *beyond this life*. These tensions are resolved in the new covenant promised by Jeremiah, which will be the subject of Chapter 3.

### *The Unconditional Covenant with Abraham*

After the expulsion from Eden and the story of the flood, people were dispersed over the earth. God reached out to establish a covenant with Abraham (whose name at the time was still "Abram"):

> Now the Lord said to Abram, "Go from your country and your kindred and your father's house to the land that I will show you. I will make of you a great nation, and I will bless you, and make your name great, so that you will be a blessing. I will bless those who bless you, and the one who curses you I will curse; *and in you all the families of the earth shall be blessed.*" (Genesis 12:1-3, NRSV, my emphasis)

God's intent, in establishing this covenant, is to create a people who will begin to reflect the special closeness God had hoped to enjoy with Adam and Eve in the garden, and eventually "to bless all the families of the earth." The only condition is that Abram must separate from his family of origin and go where God leads. When God renews the covenant with Abraham (Genesis 17:1-14), the only additional requirement is that Abraham and his male heirs carry the sign of circumcision.

This covenant required nothing ethically of the patriarchs, and their lives reflect that liberty. Consider, for instance, the self-serving lies of Abraham (Genesis 12:12-13), the drunken incest of Lot (Genesis 19:30ff), the deceitful thievery of Jacob (Genesis 27), the magical divination practiced by Joseph (Genesis 44:5). In each of these cases (and there are many others) the patriarchs lived in ways that were contrary to requirements God would later express in the covenant with Moses. But the covenant with Abraham had no conditions. It was a covenant of unmerited love—a covenant of grace—with a people who were defined solely by kinship with Abraham, the one whom God had called. God simply announced: "I have chosen you; I will bless you, and through you others will be blessed."

Of course, God had not changed character; it wasn't that God no longer cared how people acted—whether people chose "good" or "evil." That would imply a cold indifference to human suffering on the part of God. On the contrary, the scripture says that God expected Abraham to teach his family righteousness and justice (Genesis 18:19). But, perhaps to underline that the covenant was based on God's own desire to save rather than on the chosen people's prior goodness, the covenant with Abraham made no reference to ethical requirements. This is the essential background to Paul's later claim in the fourth chapter of his Letter to the Romans that Chris-

tians are the spiritual children of Abraham: they are justified
before God by faith in God's goodness, not by a righteousness
of their own.

## The Covenant of Law with Moses

When the tribes of Abraham were brought out of Egypt
into the land of promise, God established a covenant with
Moses that had quite a different character. It required the re-
ciprocating obedience of the people in both ritual and ethics.
Of course, this covenant remains an expression of God's love.
Indeed, the law is itself an act of love—for the law instructs
us how to live in communion with God and, if the law cannot in the end make us holy, it does, at the very least, limit the
violence and oppression of life outside of Eden. Therefore, the
people of faith sing:

> The law of the Lord is perfect,
>   reviving the soul;
> the decrees of the Lord are sure,
>   making wise the simple;
> the precepts of the Lord are right,
>   rejoicing the heart;
> the commandment of the Lord is clear,
>   enlightening the eyes;
> the fear of the Lord is pure,
>   enduring forever;
> the ordinances of the Lord are true
>   and righteous altogether.
> More to be desired are they than gold,
>   even much fine gold;
> sweeter also than honey,
>   and drippings of the honeycomb.
> Moreover by them is your servant warned;
>   in keeping them there is great reward.
> (Psalm 19:7-11, NRSV)

It is in the story of Moses that the Bible first introduces the language of salvation. Many words are used for the saving work of God, but the primary word in Hebrew is *yasha*. The first two occurrences of *yasha* in scripture appear in the Exodus story.

Moses was a Hebrew child who had grown up in the court of Pharaoh. One day he encountered an Egyptian soldier abusing some Hebrew slaves, and he was outraged. In anger, Moses struck and killed the soldier. When this became known at court, he feared for his life and fled to the land of Midian. As he was sitting by a well, he observed the seven daughters of the priest of Midian getting water for their father's flock.

> Some shepherds came along and drove them away,
> but Moses got up and came to their rescue/*yasha*
> and watered their flock. (Exodus 2:17, NIV)

Aside from the fact that Moses later married one of the women he rescued that day, the story is important for providing the first use of the word *yasha* in the Bible. In Moses' assault on the Egyptian soldier and in his rescue/*yasha* of the women from the shepherds, we see Moses attempting to save people by his own means and power.

This fight at the well comes shortly before the turning point in Moses' life when God called to him out of the burning bush. There, he was instructed by God to return to Egypt, confront Pharaoh, and lead the Hebrew people out into the desert. They were trapped by Pharaoh's army at the Red Sea, and this is the occasion of the second occurrence of the word *yasha*. *Yasha*—this time Divine salvation rather than a human substitute—is the word the Bible uses to summarize what God did to save the people from Pharaoh's army. It is worth reading the entirety of the Bible's first account of God acting to save his people:

> Then Moses stretched out his hand over the sea. The Lord drove the sea back by a strong east wind all night, and turned the sea into dry land; and the waters were divided. The Israelites went into the sea on dry ground, the waters forming a wall for them on their right and on their left. The Egyptians pursued, and went into the sea after them, all of Pharaoh's horses, chariots, and chariot drivers.
>
> At the morning watch the Lord in the pillar of fire and cloud looked down upon the Egyptian army, and threw the Egyptian army into panic. He clogged their chariot wheels so that they turned with difficulty. The Egyptians said, "Let us flee from the Israelites, for the Lord is fighting for them against Egypt."
>
> Then the Lord said to Moses, "Stretch out your hand over the sea, so that the water may come back upon the Egyptians, upon their chariots and chariot drivers."
>
> So Moses stretched out his hand over the sea, and at dawn the sea returned to its normal depth. As the Egyptians fled before it, the Lord tossed the Egyptians into the sea. The waters returned and covered the chariots and the chariot drivers, the entire army of Pharaoh that had followed them into the sea; not one of them remained. But the Israelites walked on dry ground through the sea, the waters forming a wall for them on their right and on their left.
>
> Thus the Lord saved/*wayasha* Israel that day from the Egyptians; and Israel saw the Egyptians dead on the seashore. (Exodus 14:21-30, NRSV)

This is the event that initially defined salvation for Judaism: God's very physical intervention on behalf of the Hebrew people to save them from their enemies and rescue them from oppression.

In the opening words of the Ten Commandments, God offers this self-definition:

> Then God spoke all these words: I am the Lord your God, who brought you out of the land of Egypt, out of the house of slavery; you shall have no other gods before me. (Exodus 20:1-3; Deuteronomy 5:5-7, NRSV)

Having defined himself as the God who saves in this specific way, God goes on to specify the terms of this covenant. It is a covenant that requires obedience of the people of God to the laws of God:

> Moses convened all Israel, and said to them: Hear, O Israel, the statutes and ordinances that I am addressing to you today; you shall learn them and observe them diligently. The Lord our God made a covenant with us at Horeb.... And he said: ... I the Lord your God am a jealous God, punishing children for the iniquity of parents, to the third and fourth generation of those who reject me, but showing steadfast love to the thousandth generation of those who love me and keep my commandments. (Deuteronomy 5:1-3, 9-10, NRSV; cf., Exodus 20:1-17)

The themes of obedience to the statutes and commandments (e.g., Exodus 15:26; 20:5; Leviticus 22:31-33; 26:3-6, 14-18; Deuteronomy 6:1-5 and passim), of being holy to the Lord and thus separated from the impure and unethical ways of the world (e.g., Leviticus 11:44-45; 19:2-19) are of the essence of the covenant with Moses. The ethical laws point to the life God intended in creation, and the religious laws draw the heart to relationship with the living God. It is a conditional covenant, a covenant of law and truth, by which God tries to draw humanity into goodness.

### *The Everlasting Covenant with David*

From the days when God rescued them from slavery in Egypt and brought them into the promised land, God continued to save the people from their enemies. Initially, the people were ruled by prophets like Moses who were anointed by God to serve as "judges" over the people. Their primary function was to deliver the people from their enemies. During their initial invasion of Canaan

> the Lord raised up judges, who saved them out of the hands of these raiders. (Judges 2:16, NIV)

Samuel was the last such judge, and at God's command he anointed Saul to be king:

> Samuel took a vial of oil and poured it on his head, and kissed him; he said, "The Lord has anointed you ruler over his people Israel. You shall reign over the people of the Lord and you will save them from the hand of their enemies all around. (1 Samuel 10:1-2, NRSV)

Samuel also gave him a sign—he would be filled with the spirit in a prophetic frenzy:

> Now this shall be the sign to you that the Lord has anointed you ruler over his heritage: . . . you will meet a band of prophets coming down from the shrine with harp, tambourine, flute, and lyre playing

in front of them; they will be in a prophetic frenzy. Then the spirit of the Lord will possess you, and you will be in a prophetic frenzy along with them and be turned into a different person. . . . Therefore it became a proverb, "Is Saul also among the prophets?" (1 Samuel 10:6-7, NRSV)

In this way Saul became the perfect bridge from the rule of the judges who were prophets to the rule of the kings who were not prophets but were advised by them. Although the form had changed, God's purpose to save the people continued the same:

> Through my servant David I will save my people Israel from the hand of the Philistines, and from all their enemies." (2 Samuel 3:18b, NRSV)

The transition from the judges to the kings culminated in the covenant with King David. When David thought he would be the one to build a house for the Lord, the prophet Nathan rebuked him, and said that, instead, God would establish David's house. It would be David's son who would be allowed to build a temple for God. Nathan concluded that prophetic word with the astonishing promise that David's line would be "eternal":

> Thus says the Lord of hosts: I took you from the pasture, from following the sheep to be prince over my people Israel; and I have been with you wherever you went, and have cut off all your enemies from before you. . . . When your days are fulfilled and you lie down with your ancestors, I will raise up your offspring after you, who shall come forth from your body, and I will establish his kingdom. He shall build a house for my name, and I will establish the throne of his kingdom forever. (2 Samuel 7:8-9, 12-13a, NRSV)

So God established the "everlasting covenant" with David (2 Samuel 23:5) that eventually became the wellspring of the Messianic hope. In the promise given through the prophet Nathan, God united salvation from enemies with the preservation of the kingdom. Even though the promise that David's kingdom would be everlasting was unconditional, Nathan made clear that the ethical requirements of the Mosaic covenant were still in force:

> When he commits iniquity, I will punish him with a rod such as mortals use, with blows inflicted by human beings. But I will not take my steadfast love from him.... (2 Samuel 7:14-15, NRSV)

Indeed, Nathan was not hesitant to chastise David himself. When David engineered the death of Uriah so that David could marry Uriah's wife, Bathsheba, Nathan's condemnation was withering (See 2 Samuel 12:1-12.). David's greatness was that he accepted the criticism with a humble spirit:

> [To the leader. A Psalm of David, when the prophet Nathan came to him, after he had gone in to Bathsheba.]
>
> Have mercy on me, O God,
>   according to your steadfast love;
> according to your abundant mercy
>   blot out my transgressions.
> Wash me thoroughly from my iniquity,
>   and cleanse me from my sin.
> . . . . . . . . . . . . . . . . . . . . . . . . .
> Create in me a clean heart, O God,
>   and put a new and right spirit within me.
> Do not cast me away from your presence,
>   and do not take your holy spirit from me.

Restore to me the joy of your salvation,
and sustain in me a willing spirit.
(Psalm 51:1-2, 10-12, NRSV)

## The Covenant Broken

David's kingdom—at least in its political form—soon began to crack, and it eventually fell. The story of that collapse is the burden of the books of Kings, Chronicles, and the prophets.

In Second Chronicles, the story is told of how Solomon succeeded to his father David's throne and filled the court in Jerusalem with wealth.

> The weight of gold that came to Solomon in one year was six hundred sixty-six talents of gold, besides that which the traders and merchants brought; and all the kings of Arabia and the governors of the land brought gold and silver to Solomon. . . .
>
> All the kings of the earth sought the presence of Solomon to hear his wisdom, which God had put into his mind. Every one of them brought a present, objects of silver and gold, garments, weaponry, spices, horses, and mules, so much year by year. Solomon had four thousand stalls for horses and chariots, and twelve thousand horses, which he stationed in the chariot cities and with the king in Jerusalem.
>
> He ruled over all the kings from the Euphrates to the land of the Philistines, and to the border of Egypt. The king made silver as common in Jerusalem as stone, and cedar as plentiful as the sycamore of the Shephelah. (2 Chronicles 9:13-14, 23-27, NRSV)

His palace also became a harem: "Among his wives were seven hundred princesses and three hundred concubines" (1

Kings 11:3a, NRSV), and in the midst of all this luxury, in a sad commentary on the corrupting power of wealth, Solomon abandoned wisdom and his heart turned away from God:

> Solomon followed Astarte the goddess of the Sidnians, and Milcom the abomination of the Ammonites. (1 Kings 11:5, NRSV)

Reared in this atmosphere of luxury and spiritual confusion, is it any wonder that Solomon's children showed a tyrannical spirit when they came to the throne? After his coronation, Rehoboam, Solomon's son, rejected the advice of the older courtiers to "lighten the hard service of your father and his heavy yoke," but instead followed the counsel of "the young men who had grown up with him" and announced,

> "Now, whereas my father laid on you a heavy yoke,
> I will add to your yoke. My father disciplined you
> with whips, but I will discipline you with scorpions."
> (2 Chronicles 10:4, passim, NRSV)

This provoked a rebellion, and the northern kingdom of Israel severed itself from the southern kingdom of Judah.

The prophets continually cried out warnings to the people that, when the nation tolerated injustice, they were betraying not only the poor but God. God speaks to the people through Amos:

> Thus says the Lord:
> For three transgressions of Israel, and for four,
>     I will not revoke the punishment;
> because they sell the righteous for silver,
>     and the needy for a pair of sandals—
> they who trample the head of the poor into the
>     dust of the earth,

and push the afflicted out of the way;
father and son go in to the same girl,
    so that my holy name is profaned;
they lay themselves down beside every altar
    on garments taken in pledge;
and in the house of their God they drink
    wine bought with fines they imposed.
(Amos 2:6-8, NRSV)

The prophets warned, again and again, that true worship of God means a life devoted to justice. This is of the essence of the covenant that God proclaimed through Moses:

I hate, I despise your festivals,
    and I take no delight in your solemn assemblies.
Even though you offer me your burnt offerings
    and grain offerings,
    I will not accept them;
and the offerings of well-being of your fatted
    animals
    I will not look upon.
Take away from me the noise of your songs;
    I will not listen to the melody of your harps.
But let justice roll down like waters,
    and righteousness like an ever-flowing stream.
(Amos 5:21-24, NRSV)

The message is that the ethical corruption of the kingdom of God betrays the basic covenant of salvation that lies at the heart of God's choice of a people who will be a blessing to the nations. God pleads with the people, "Seek good and not evil, that you may live. . . ." (Amos 5:14a, NRSV)

God will not—perhaps, cannot—tolerate injustice and oppression forever, for it is God's nature to save. Amos warns the elite of the northern kingdom of Israel that their kingdom will be taken from them. Addressing the women, he says:

> Hear this word, you cows of Bashan
>   who are on Mount Samaria,
> who oppress the poor, who crush the needy,
>   who say to their husbands, "Bring something to
>     drink!"
> The Lord God has sworn by his holiness:
>   The time is surely coming upon you,
> when they shall take you away with hooks,
>   even the last of you with fishhooks.
> Through breaches in the wall you shall leave,
>   each one straight ahead;
> and you shall be flung out into Harmon, says the
>     Lord.
>                                (Amos 4:1-3, NRSV)

Shortly after the time of Amos, the prophet Hosea declared the awful judgment that the covenant had been broken and that the kingdom of Israel would be destroyed:

> Set the trumpet to your lips!
>   One like a vulture is over the house of the Lord,
> because they have broken my covenant,
>   and transgressed my law.
>                                (Hosea 8:1, NRSV)

Within a generation the northern kingdom was no more. It fell in 722 B.C., before the assault of Shalmaneser V of Assyria.

The southern kingdom of Judah—even with the Temple worship at Jerusalem at its center—was no more successful in fulfilling its covenant obligations. Jeremiah expresses his own, and God's, anguish:

> Run to and fro through the streets of Jerusalem,
>   look around and take note!
> Search its squares and see

48

if you can find one person
who acts justly and seeks truth—
so that I may pardon Jerusalem.

Although they say, "As the Lord lives," yet they
    swear falsely.
O Lord, do your eyes not look for truth?
You have struck them,
    but they felt no anguish;
you have consumed them,
    but they refused to take correction.
They have made their faces harder than rock;
    they have refused to turn back.
. . . . . . . . . . . . . . . . . . . . . . . . . . . . .
For scoundrels are found among my people;
    they take over the goods of others.
Like fowlers they set a trap;
    they catch human beings.
Like a cage full of birds,
    their houses are full of treachery;
therefore they have become great and rich,
    they have grown fat and sleek.
They know no limits in deeds of wickedness;
    they do not judge with justice
the cause of the orphan, to make it prosper,
    and they do not defend the rights of the needy.
Shall I not punish them for these things?
        says the Lord,
    and shall I not bring retribution on a nation
        such as this?
                                (Jeremiah 5:1-3, 23-29, NRSV)

Finally, it became Jeremiah's awful task to announce the destruction of the southern kingdom, Judah. Speaking through
Jeremiah, God brings this indictment:

They have turned back to the iniquities of their ancestors of old, who refused to heed my words; they

> have gone after other gods to serve them; the house
> of Israel and the house of Judah have broken the
> covenant that I made with their ancestors. (Jeremi-
> ah 11:10, NRSV)

Imagine Jeremiah's anguish in announcing the destruction of the kingdom that earlier prophets had proclaimed to be an "everlasting kingdom" (e.g., Jeremiah 4:10, 19-20; 7:3-15). Within a few years of this announcement, in 586 B.C., Jeru-salem fell to Nebuchadrezzar, and the Temple was destroyed. When God declared that the covenant was broken, the world saw the destruction of the kingdoms. Here is God's assertion that there can be no salvation without justice and righteous-ness.

## The Day of Judgment

All through the six hundred years of the judges and the kings, God had continued to call to the people through various prophets and leaders, and most of all through the instruction of Torah (the first five books of scripture), to return to the way of life God intended from the beginning. When they did not, there came times of oppression, followed by repentance and a new saving act of God. The destruction of the kingdoms and the exile of the leaders introduced a new understanding of how God might act. The prophets began to foretell a time when evil in the land would become so great that God would appear in power to set things straight. This would not be part of the normal cycle of history but a judgment of cosmic pro-portion. They called this the day of the Lord's visitation.

That day, they said, will be "the day of punishment" (Isaiah 10:3) and "retribution" (Jeremiah 46:10), coming "like destruc-tion from the Almighty" (Isaiah 13:6). It will be "a day of dark-ness and gloom" (Joel 2:1), "burning like an oven" (Malachi

4:1). God warned against the day: "Thus says the Lord God: Wail, 'Alas for the day!'" (Ezekiel 30:3).

Amos was eloquent in chiding those who sought their vindication on the day of the Lord:

> Alas for you who desire the day of the Lord!
>   Why do you want the day of the Lord?
> It is darkness, not light;
>   as if someone fled from a lion, and was met
>     by a bear;
>   or went into the house and rested a hand against
>     the wall,
>   and was bitten by a snake.
> Is not the day of the Lord darkness, not light,
>   and gloom with no brightness in it?
>                         (Amos 5:18-20, NRSV)

Among the prophets of the day of the Lord, Zephaniah was preeminent in summing up its terror:

> The great day of the Lord is near,
>   near and hastening fast;
> the sound of the day of the Lord is bitter,
>   the warrior cries aloud there.
> That day will be a day of wrath,
>   a day of distress and anguish,
> a day of ruin and devastation,
>   a day of darkness and gloom,
> a day of clouds and thick darkness,
>   a day of trumpet blast and battle cry
> against the fortified cities
>   and against the lofty battlements.
> I will bring such distress upon people
>   that they shall walk like the blind;
>   because they have sinned against the Lord,
> their blood shall be poured out like dust,
>   and their flesh like dung.
>                         (Zephaniah 1:14-17, NRSV)

Whether the day is to be visited upon Judah or Israel or "the nations," the point was always the same: the moment will come when God will act decisively to set things straight.

The breaking of the covenant and the destruction of the kingdoms of Israel and Judah was just such a day of visitation. The exile in Babylon was a time of solemn reevaluation of what it meant to be the people of God, and of how God saves. The second part of the book of Isaiah appeared at this time with its profound conceptualization of the nation of Israel in exile as the chastised servant of God who has suffered for the sins of the people but who will be restored and bring about the justice that had been lost:

> Here is my servant, whom I uphold,
>   my chosen, in whom my soul delights;
> I have put my spirit upon him;
>   he will bring forth justice to the nations.
> He will not cry or lift up his voice,
>   or make it heard in the street;
> a bruised reed he will not break,
>   and a dimly burning wick he will not quench;
> he will faithfully bring forth justice.
> He will not grow faint or be crushed
> until he has established justice in the earth;
>   and the coastlands wait for his teaching.
>                   (Isaiah 42:1-4, NRSV;
>                   see also, Isaiah 52:13-15
>                   and Isaiah 53:4-6)

The books of Ezra and Nehemiah, together with the prophetic collections of Zechariah, Haggai and Malachi, detail the return to Judah and the rebuilding of the Temple. During this period, as the breadth of vision of the prophets increasingly conflicts with the limited justice and righteousness that they see around them, they begin to express the hope for the realization of the kingdom of God in "apocalyptic" terms. In apocalyptic writing, the prophet sees beyond ordinary history to a coming age and a new creation. God instructs the prophet Haggai:

> Speak to Zerubbabel, governor of Judah, saying, I am about to shake the heavens and the earth, and to overthrow the throne of kingdoms; I am about to destroy the strength of the kingdoms of the nations. . . . (Haggai 2:21-22a, NRSV)

Zechariah has an expanded vision of a new and final day of the Lord:

> See, a day is coming for the Lord, when the plunder taken from you will be divided in your midst. . . . On that day there shall not be either cold or frost. And there shall be continuous day (it is known to the Lord), not day and not night, for at evening time there shall be light. On that day living waters shall flow out from Jerusalem, half of them to the eastern sea and half of them to the western sea; it shall continue in summer as in winter. And the Lord will become king over all the earth; on that day the Lord will be one and his name one. (Zechariah 14:1, 6-7, NRSV)

In the final portion of the book of Isaiah, God brings this vision to completion:

> For I am about to create new heavens
>   and a new earth;
> the former things shall not be remembered
>   or come to mind.
> But be glad and rejoice forever
>   in what I am creating;

for I am about to create Jerusalem as a joy,
and its people as a delight.
. . . . . . . . . . . . . . . . . . . . . . . .
Before they call I will answer,
while they are yet speaking I will hear.
The wolf and the lamb shall feed together,
the lion shall eat straw like the ox;
but the serpent—its food shall be dust!
They shall not hurt or destroy
on all my holy mountain, says the Lord.
(Isaiah 65: 17-18, 24-26, NRSV)

The relative independence of Judah as a vassal state following the exile ended in 333 B.C. in the great disaster of the world-conquest of Alexander the Great of Greece. Alexander's successors, the Seleucid dynasty, attempted to obliterate the Jewish faith and replace Jewish culture with Greek commercial culture including their pantheon of gods and goddesses. The force and cruelty they employed were overwhelming; the story of the Jewish resistance is the subject of the books of Maccabees.

This experience of extreme repression heightened Jewish expectation that God's salvation would come with cataclysmic force. The hope was increasingly expressed in apocalyptic language based in Isaiah's vision of a new heaven and a new earth. Many began to believe during this time that salvation would be found in a resurrection life beyond the grave.[2] One such expression, from the Second Book of Maccabees, is the defiant speech of one of seven brothers who is dying under torture. The faithful Jew declaims to his Seleucid oppressor:

> "You accursed wretch, you dismiss us from this present life, but the King of the universe will raise us up to an everlasting renewal of life, because we have died for his laws." (2 Maccabees 7:9, NRSV; cf., 12:43-44)

The anonymous book 1 Enoch, dating from this same period, elaborated on this theme. Here is a typical passage:

> In those days, there will be a change for the holy and righteous ones and the light of days shall rest upon them. . . .
>
> In those days, Sheol will return all the deposits which she had received and hell will give back all that which it owes. And [God] shall choose the righteous and the holy ones from among them, for the day when they shall be selected and saved has arrived. . . .
>
> And the faces of all the angels in heaven shall glow with joy, because on that day the Elect One has arisen. And the earth shall rejoice; and the righteous ones shall dwell upon her and the elect ones shall walk upon her. (1 Enoch 50:1; 51:1-2, 4-5)[3]

This hope in a Messiah ("the Elect One") who will usher in a day of resurrection in which the righteous will be saved to enjoy everlasting life became a central feature of Christianity.

In Jesus' day, Judaism was engaged in a great argument between those who did and those who did not accept this hope that the righteous would experience resurrection on the day of the Lord. Jesus, with the Pharisees, accepted the hope of resurrection and argued against those, like the Sadducees, who held that at death the faithful simply die (Cf., Matthew 22:23; Mark 12:18; Luke 20:27; Acts 23:8). He argued strenuously that the faithful "dead" will live in the coming resurrection:

> Have you not read in the book of Moses, in the story about the bush, how God said to him, 'I am the God of Abraham, the God of Isaac, and the God of Jacob'? He is God not of the dead, but of the living; you are quite wrong." (Mark 12:26b-27, NRSV; cf., Matthew 22:32; Luke 20:38)

As in the Old Testament, the New Testament understanding is that people "fall asleep" in death. Now the expectation is that they "sleep" awaiting an ultimate awakening in a bodily resurrection.[4] Jesus prefigured this with his friend Lazarus:

> "Our friend Lazarus has fallen asleep, but I am going there [to his graveside] to awaken him." (John 11:11, NRSV)

Lazarus' resurrection was a sign of the general resurrection to come:

> The hour is coming when all who are in their graves will hear his voice and will come out—those who have done good, to the resurrection of life, and those who have done evil, to the resurrection of condemnation. (John 5:28b-29, NRSV)

Hope in resurrection alters the biblical understanding of salvation, but does not fundamentally change it. Salvation, which was first pictured in terms of God's deliverance from human oppressors, has now expanded to include safe passage through the time when God will come in final judgment to usher in the new heaven and new earth of the resurrection.

The New Testament is full of anticipation of this day of God's judgment. Jesus spoke of the coming day—a prospect of "fire where there will be weeping and gnashing of teeth" for those who do evil (Matthew 13:41-43, NRSV; cf. Matthew 5:22; 10:15; 12:34-37; 18:8-9; Luke 17:24-35, etc.), as did Paul (Romans 2:16; 1 Corinthians 5:5; 1 Thessalonians 5:1-5; 2 Thessalonians 1:6-10; 2:1-3), the author of Hebrews (Hebrews 10:26-27), and Peter (2 Peter 2:7-10). Even John—in the same letter in which he says, "God is love,"—looked forward to that day: "Love has been perfected among us in this:

that we may have boldness on the day of judgment..." (1 John 4:17, NRSV).

God's ultimate purpose is to restore people to the goodness God intended in the creation. The covenant of Moses, with its loving provision of the law, had been broken. Now, God's same intention is expressed in the expectation of the resurrection of the righteous. From Enoch to the Book of Revelation, it is the righteous who will enjoy the resurrection, not the wicked. Enoch writes of God's judgment:

> He heaped evil upon the sinners; but the righteous ones shall be victorious in the name of the Lord of the Spirits. . . . He is righteous in his judgment and in the glory that is before him. Oppression cannot survive his judgment; and the unrepentant in his presence shall perish. The Lord of the Spirits has said that from henceforth he will not have mercy on them. (1 Enoch 50: 2,4-5)[5]

John describes his vision of the New Jerusalem in the same terms:

> Nothing accursed will be found there any more. But the throne of God and of the Lamb will be in it, and his servants will worship him. . . . (Revelation 22:3, NRSV)

Paul shared this expectation that the resurrection hope was tied to ethics. In his writing, Paul often distinguishes between something he calls "justification" and "salvation":

> But God proves his love for us in that while we still were sinners Christ died for us. Much more surely then, now that we *have been justified* by his blood, *will we be saved* through him from the wrath of God.

> For if while we were enemies, we were reconciled to
> God through the death of his Son, much more sure-
> ly, *having been reconciled, will we be saved* by his life.
> (Romans 5:8-10, NRSV, my emphasis; c.f, 1 Thes-
> salonians 5:9; 2 Timothy 4:18)

For Paul, justification—being made "just" or "righteous" by the forgiveness of God—comes by the grace of God. It is the dec-laration by God of the forgiveness of sin. Justification stands at the beginning of the believer's life with God (thus his use of the past tense) and leads to salvation on the future day of judg-ment, when "we will be saved . . . from the wrath of God."[6] Jus-tification makes possible the righteousness that God requires on that day when he will save the righteous and bring them into the resurrection of life.

Because the Apostle Paul emphasized that we have been justified by faith alone, some misunderstood him to say that we will ultimately be saved whether or not our lives actually reflect genuine righteousness. Peter was alarmed about this confusion, fearing that the Christians of his time would feel free to live "lawless" lives and endanger their salvation. He wrote this warning:

> But the day of the Lord will come like a thief, and
> then the heavens will pass away with a loud noise,
> and the elements will be dissolved with fire, and the
> earth and everything that is done on it will be dis-
> closed.
>
> Since all these things are to be dissolved in this way,
> what sort of persons ought you to be in leading lives
> of holiness and godliness, waiting for and hastening
> the coming of the day of God, because of which the
> heavens will be set ablaze and dissolved, and the ele-
> ments will melt with fire? But, in accordance with his

promise, we wait for new heavens and a new earth, where righteousness is at home. Therefore, beloved, while you are waiting for these things, strive to be found by him at peace, without spot or blemish; and regard the patience of our Lord as salvation.

So also our beloved brother Paul wrote to you according to the wisdom given him, speaking of this as he does in all his letters. There are some things in them hard to understand, which the ignorant and unstable twist to their own destruction, as they do the other scriptures. You therefore, beloved, since you are forewarned, beware that you are not carried away with the error of the lawless and lose your own stability. (2 Peter 3:10-17, NRSV)

The requirement of righteousness raises a profound dilemma for those who hope to experience God's salvation. How can people attain the genuine righteousness that is necessary for salvation "on that day," when we have proven so definitively incapable of it that God declared the covenant of the law to be broken? This dilemma was resolved on the cross, when Jesus inaugurated the new covenant promised by God through Jeremiah.

---

[1] To attempt a comprehensive understanding of what the scripture means by "save" and "salvation," I used a computer concordance to identify all the verses where variants of save/*sozo* and salvation/*soteria* appeared in the Greek New Testament and the Septuagint (LXX)—the translation of the Old Testament into Greek that was current in the years leading up to the New Testament period.

I assume that the NT writers would have been particularly informed by LXX usage. Evidence for that includes the fact that Hebrews 8:12 cites the LXX—rather than the Hebrew—version of the new covenant passage, thus introducing the word mercy ("I will be merciful toward their iniquities"), where the Hebrew of Jeremiah 31:34 reads, "I will forgive their iniquity."

In the following examples, Paul and Peter quote from the LXX version rather than the Hebrew; their quotations use the language of salvation introduced by the LXX where comparable words are not even present in the Hebrew.

The Hebrew reads:

> If the righteous are repaid on earth, how much more the wicked and the sinner! (Proverbs 11:31, NRSV)

but the LXX has:

> If the righteous be scarcely saved, what shall become of the ungodly and the sinner?"

and 1 Peter 4:18 follows the LXX.

Whereas the Hebrew reads:

> For though your people Israel were like the sand of the sea, only a remnant of them will return. Destruction is decreed, overflowing with righteousness. (Isaiah 10:22, NRSV)

The LXX reads that a remnant of them "shall be saved" instead of "will return." Paul quotes the LXX version in Romans 9:27. It seems clear to me that the New Testament writers understood the words for salvation according to the Greek version of the scripture.

Altogether, I looked at 753 verses (579 in the Old Testament and 174 in the New Testament) where some variation of *sozo* and *soterian* appear. I attempted to determine the meaning of terms by their context. Sometimes the meanings were ambiguous and no doubt other readers would understand particular uses differently than I. Thus, the percentages that I have assigned to different connotations are only approximations.

In the LXX, *sozo* and *soterion* translated a good number of Hebrew words. The roots *yasha* and *yeshua* are by far the most frequent, occurring 212 times. Other words translated this way significantly often were *malat*, *natsal*, and variations on *palet* all of which are frequently rendered in English versions as "deliver" and "escape." In addition, there are 69 verses in which *soterian* is employed in the LXX for *shalom*. Without exception, these concern what the KJV translates as "peace offering," NIV the "fellowship offering," and NRSV "sacrifice of well-being." I take it that this sacrifice concerns the prosperity of the community, and that the LXX, in these instances, understands salvation in the light of economics.

Of the 753 verses, 127 verses (17% in the OT and 2% in the NT) concern human-originated acts. It is worth noting that more than half of these instances carry the sense of "escape" from some sort of danger, and by far most of the rest concern military victory or deliverance from danger.

The remaining 626 verses concern the saving activity of God. In the Old Testament, 62% concern physical safety from danger or victory in war. The next largest category (15%) was the offering of *shalom*. The remaining quarter were scattered among forgiveness of sin, the faithful remnant, economic provision, justice for the poor, health, and passages where the usage was not identifiable.

In this regard, the New Testament was almost a reverse image of the Old, with 50% of the usage being indefinable or referring to forgiveness of sin. This compares with 6% in this category in the OT. Two other large categories concern God's safe deliverance of believers through the cataclysm of the end times (15% as compared to 2% in the OT) and physical healing (12% of the NT compared to 2% in the OT). The remainder were scattered much as in the OT.

One of the most interesting findings concerns Jesus' use of the terminology of salvation. Of 25 verses where Jesus is quoted using one of these words, 16% concern safety on the day of judgment, and 44% deal with physical healing. (These figures, of course, reflect the repetition of the synoptic Gospels.)

This analysis suggests that salvation originally meant the creation of a place of safety from the dangers of this world through the intervention of God. As the hope of Israel began to take the form of a day of judgment followed by a new heaven and new earth, salvation came to mean God's protection of the faithful in the time of judgment and their safe conveyance into the resurrection life. Jesus evidently saw himself as not only announcing the imminent arrival of that day of judgment, but as also bringing that experience of salvation into people's lives through his healing ministry during their earthly lives.

² Daniel 12:1-2 and Isaiah 26:19 contain the only unambiguous expression of hope in the resurrection in the Old Testament. Daniel was probably written during the reign of Antiochus IV (175-163 B.C.) and was part of the outpouring of apocalyptic literature that included such non-canonical writings as 1 Enoch. The Isaiah passage is part of a section of Isaiah called by some scholars, "The Little Apocalypse," and likely dates from the same period.

³ In Charlesworth, *op cit.*

⁴ Although heaven and hell have come to dominate popular Christian expectations of what salvation is about, in the Bible these terms are not associated with "salvation" nor do they feature prominently in the expectation for what follows death. "Sheol" (the word sometimes translated as "hell" in the Old Testament) simply means the grave, the pit where the body was placed at death, decomposed, and was eaten by worms (cf., Job 17:12ff). The predominant expectation in the Old Testament is that death is final.

> The dead do not praise the LORD,
> nor do any that go down into silence.
> (Psalm 115:17, NRSV)

While Jesus uses the imagery of heaven and hell to make forceful points, he does not forecast that people will live in either place after they die. Throughout the Bible, "heaven" is the dwelling place of God, angels, and the host of heaven, but it is not the home for people in "the afterlife." There is one exception to this rule in both the Old and the New Testaments. In the case of Elijah, it is said that at the end of his life he "ascended . . . into heaven" (2 Kings 2:11, NRSV). In Luke, Jesus promises those being crucified beside him, "today you will be with me in Paradise" (Luke 23:43, NRSV). Otherwise, in the New Testament, the expectation is that Christians will "fall asleep" in hope of the resurrection (see Matthew 27:52; Acts 7:60; 13:36; 1 Corinthians 7:39; 11:30; 15:6-20; 1 Thessalonians 4:13-15; 2 Peter 3:4; and perhaps Mark 12:25).

Jesus is frequently spoken of as dwelling in heaven beside the throne of God as he awaits his second coming, but for the rest of us, the hope is not in a spiritual state (or location) called "heaven" but for a new life in the bodily resurrection. Paul makes the distinction clear:

> For the Lord himself, with a cry of command, with the archangel's call and with the sound of God's trumpet, will descend from heaven, and the dead in Christ will rise first. (1 Thessalonians 4:16, NRSV)

Jesus will come down "from heaven," and the dead believers will rise up—from the grave! John makes the categorical claim:

> No one has ascended into heaven except the one who descended from heaven, the Son of Man. (John 3:13, NRSV; cf., Acts 2:34)

⁵ In Charlesworth, *op cit.*

⁶ Paul sometimes places God's saving action in the future, sometimes in the past, and sometimes in the continuing experience of the believer. There are 31 occurrences of the verb save/ *sozo* in Paul's letters. Of these, there are eleven occasions (including the verses just quoted) when Paul is anticipating a future event when believers "will be saved" at the final judgment. For instance:

> If the work is burned up, the builder will suffer loss; the builder will be saved, but only as through fire. (1 Corinthians 3:15, NRSV; cf., 1 Corinthians 5:5; Romans 5:9-10; 9:27; 11:14, 26; 2 Thessalonians 2:10; 1 Timothy 1:15; 2:4)

However, Paul also writes of God saving believers in their present experience in the sense of God rescuing believers from danger. In the Second Letter to Timothy Paul anticipates the saving work of God in this way:

> The Lord will rescue me from every evil attack and save me for his heavenly kingdom. To him be the glory forever and ever. Amen. (2 Timothy 4:18, NRSV)

Thus, Paul retains the Old Testament understanding of salvation as including rescue from danger. There are four additional occasions when Paul writes of believers "who are being saved," as if salvation is a continuing event unfolding in their lives. Using the present passive, Paul writes:

> For the message about the cross is foolishness to those who are perishing, but to us who are being saved it is the power of God. (1 Corinthians 1:18, NRSV; cf., 1 Corinthians 15:2; 2 Corinthians 2:15)

Unless Paul has suddenly decided that women can "earn" their spiritual salvation, the verse about women being saved "through" childbirth,

> Yet she will be saved through childbearing, provided they continue in faith and love and holiness, with modesty. (1 Timothy 2:15, NRSV)

must fall into this same category. Paul is using save/*sozo* in the sense of physical healing (see pp. 87 below) and is saying that a woman may be preserved through the dangers of childbearing and thus from the Genesis 3:16 curse of "pain" in childbirth.

Less than half of the time (14 occasions), Paul (often using the aorist or perfect tenses) writes of salvation as a completed action that has been, or *will be*, accomplished during the life of the believer by confession of faith. In these instances, the believer "has been saved." When he speaks of salvation Paul clearly has the final judgment in mind:

> because if you confess with your lips that Jesus is Lord and believe in your heart that God raised him from the dead, you will be saved. (Romans 10:9, NRSV)

and

> For, "Everyone who calls on the name of the Lord shall be saved." (Romans 10:13; cf., Romans 8:24; 1 Corinthians 1:21; Ephesians 2:5, 8; Titus 3:5; 2 Timothy 1:9, NRSV)

Paul also speaks of his preaching as saving some, which clearly implies that once a person believes, he or she is "saved" in this same sense (See 1 Corinthians 9:22; 7:16; 10:33; 1 Thessalonians 2:16; 1 Timothy 4:16). The great variety of ways in which Paul uses the terminology of salvation is a salutary warning against any narrow theology of God's saving work.

# THE NEW COVENANT

s Jeremiah came closer to announcing that the Mosaic covenant had been broken, he complained more and more about the "stubborn and rebellious heart" of the people. The heart, in biblical imagery, is not the seat of emotion but of the will—where the decision to love and obey is made—and Jeremiah perceives that the heart is so corrupt that the people *cannot* obey, even if they want to. Through Jeremiah, God says:

> The heart is devious above all else;
>   it is perverse—
> who can understand it?
> I the Lord test the mind
>   and search the heart,
> to give to all according to their ways,
>   according to the fruit of their doings.
>                 (Jeremiah 17:9-10, NRSV)

When Jeremiah says the heart is devious, perverse and beyond understanding, he foreshadows the cry of Paul, "For I do not do what I want, but I do the very thing I hate" (Romans 7:15, NRSV). Together, these verses express the most profound understanding of the human condition. Sometimes ruled by desires and compulsions that we may not understand or find impossible to control, always limited by the subjectivity of our perceptions; even when we will the good, we often choose a course that has unintended consequences for ill. At their best, "all our righteous acts are like filthy rags" (Isaiah 64:6, NIV). Again Jeremiah gives us God's words:

> For thus says the Lord:
> Your hurt is incurable,
>   your wound is grievous.
> There is no one to uphold your cause,
>   no medicine for your wound,
>   no healing for you.
> . . . . . . . . . . . . . . . . . . .
> Why do you cry out over your hurt?
>   Your pain is incurable.
>             (Jeremiah 30:12-13, 15a, NRSV)

Since God requires righteousness—the very thing that we cannot achieve because of the incurable woundedness of the human heart and will—God must intervene at a most profound level if we are ultimately to be saved. In the face of this reality, God offers a new possibility—healing for the heart, given miraculously, graciously, without our mereting it:

> For I will restore health to you,
>   and your wounds I will heal, says the Lord,
> . . . . . . . . . . . . . . . . . . . . . . . . . . . . . . . . . . .
> And you shall be my people,
>   and I will be your God.
>             (Jeremiah 30:17a, 22, NRSV)

Jeremiah's contemporary, the prophet Ezekiel, brought these words of promise from God to the exile community:

> I will give them one heart, and put a new spirit within them; I will remove the heart of stone from their

flesh and give them a heart of flesh, so that they may follow my statutes and keep my ordinances and obey them. Then they shall be my people, and I will be their God. (Ezekiel 11:19-20, NRSV)

and,

I will sprinkle clean water upon you, and you shall be clean from all your uncleannesses, and from all your idols I will cleanse you. A new heart I will give you, and a new spirit I will put within you; and I will remove from your body the heart of stone and give you a heart of flesh. I will put my spirit within you, and make you follow my statutes and be careful to observe my ordinances. Then you shall live in the land that I gave to your ancestors; and you shall be my people, and I will be your God. (Ezekiel 36:25-28, NRSV)

It is the possibility of a new heart, a new will miraculously transplanted into the human soul, that alone holds out hope for obedience to God.

This promise of a new heart is like the promise God gave Abraham, a blessing not based on human capacity for goodness or obedience but rather on God's utter graciousness. However, it is different from the covenant with Abraham in that it provides the means by which God's desire that humankind live a moral life might be fulfilled. The ethical imperative of the Mosaic covenant can now be accomplished through the radical gift of a new heart, a new *divinely implanted* human will that wills according to the will of God. In this promise grace and truth are united.

Because this promise is based on the healing of the perverted heart, the new covenant requires God to reach into the center of each individual personality. This means that the social structure of the kingdom of God is inevitably changed. It can no longer be based upon ethnicity as with the choice of Abraham and his descendents. Neither can it be located in a community that is geographically or politically defined as was the case with Israel and Judah under the judges and kings. The new covenant community must be a voluntary community of those who have accepted God's salvation by faith.[1]

Therefore, in announcing the new covenant, God makes it clear that it "will not be like the covenant that I made" before:

> The days are surely coming, says the Lord, when I will make a new covenant with the house of Israel and the house of Judah. It will not be like the covenant that I made with their ancestors when I took them by the hand to bring them out of the land of Egypt—a covenant that they broke, though I was their husband, says the Lord.
>
> But this is the covenant that I will make with the house of Israel after those days, says the Lord: I will put my law within them, and I will write it on their hearts; and I will be their God, and they shall be my people. No longer shall they teach one another, or say to each other, "Know the Lord," for they shall all know me, from the least of them to the greatest, says the Lord; for I will forgive their iniquity, and remember their sin no more. (Jeremiah 31:31-33, NRSV)

This is salvation indeed. Healing for the heart promises to resolve the root cause of the disobedience that resulted in humanity breaking the covenant with God. Therefore, it is possible for God to announce a new covenant in which it can be said once more: "I will be their God, and they will be my people" (Jeremiah 31:33, NRSV).

According to the scriptures, God has chosen to seal the

great covenants with blood. This was true of the covenants with Abraham and Moses; it is also true of the new covenant.

When God led Abraham out of Ur and promised to give him land and descendants who would become a blessing for all the nations, God confirmed that promise in a covenant ritual:

> [God said to Abram], "Bring me a heifer three years old, a female goat three years old, a ram three years old, a turtledove, and a young pigeon." He brought him all these and cut them in two, laying each half over against the other; but he did not cut the birds in two. And when birds of prey came down on the carcasses, Abram drove them away. As the sun was going down, a deep sleep fell upon Abram, and a deep and terrifying darkness descended upon him. . . .
>
> When the sun had gone down and it was dark, a smoking fire pot and a flaming torch passed between these pieces. On that day the Lord made a covenant with Abram. . . . (Genesis 15:9-12, 17-18a, NRSV)

When God was ready to establish the covenant with Moses, it also required blood. Moses returned to the people from the mountain after receiving the Ten Commandments and the instructions of the Law, and the people prepared a great sacrifice:

> Moses took half of the blood and put it in basins, and half of the blood he dashed against the altar. Then he took the book of the covenant, and read it in the hearing of the people; and they said, "All that the Lord has spoken we will do, and we will be obedient." Moses took the blood and dashed it on the people, and said, "See the blood of the covenant that the Lord has made with you in accordance with all these words." (Exodus 24:6-8, NRSV)

On the night during which Jesus was to be betrayed, he brought his disciples to an upper room in Jerusalem to celebrate the Passover. Jesus used the occasion to interpret his coming crucifixion to his disciples:

> He took a loaf of bread, and when he had given thanks, he broke it and gave it to them, saying, "This is my body, which is given for you. Do this in remembrance of me." And he did the same with the cup after supper, saying, "This cup that is poured out for you is the new covenant in my blood." (Luke 22:19-20, NRSV; cf., 1 Corinthians 11:24-25)

The blood that Jesus shed on the cross inaugurated the new covenant.

The Letter to the Hebrews develops this understanding of the meaning of the cross in an extended passage in which Jesus is called both "high priest" and "mediator of the new covenant":

> But when Christ came as high priest . . . he entered once for all into the sanctuary, not with the blood of goats and calves but with his own blood, thus obtaining eternal redemption. For if the blood of goats and bulls and the sprinkling of a heifer's ashes can sanctify those who are defiled so that their flesh is cleansed, how much more will the blood of Christ, who through the eternal spirit offered himself unblemished to God, cleanse our consciences from dead works to worship the living God. For this reason he is mediator of a new covenant: since a death has taken place for deliverance from transgressions under the first covenant, those who are called may receive the promised eternal inheritance. (Hebrews 9:11-15, NAB)

What is the "promised eternal inheritance"? It is eternal life—life that flows from the three promises God made to humanity in the new covenant: the forgiveness of sins, the law written inwardly on the heart, and the unmediated knowledge of the presence of God. Together, these promises are the wellspring of salvation.

### 'I will remember their sins no more.'

Forgiveness of sins frees people from the burden of guilt for the evils they have done and from bondage to wounds they have suffered when evil was done to them. Forgiveness is the first step in the transformation of hearts of stone to hearts of flesh.

Forgiveness or condemnation is the object of which God as Judge is the subject. Jesus is mediator of the new covenant not least in that he comes in the divine office of the righteous judge. A text that molds the expectation of the coming judgment of God is the account of a dream found in the book of Daniel. It formed the basis for much of the imagery of the Book of Revelation. Here is Daniel's dream:

> As I looked,
> thrones were placed
>   and one that was ancient of days took his seat;
> his raiment was white as snow,
>   and the hair of his head like pure wool;
> his throne was fiery flames,
>   its wheels were burning fire.
> A stream of fire issued
>   and came forth from before him;
> a thousand thousands served him,
>   and ten thousand times ten thousand stood before
>     him;

the court sat in judgment,
and the books were opened.
. . . . . . . . . . . . . . . . . . . . . . . . .
and behold, with the clouds of heaven
there came one like a son of man,
and he came to the Ancient of Days
and was presented before him.
And to him was given dominion
and glory and kingdom,
that all peoples, nations, and languages
should serve him;
his dominion is an everlasting dominion,
which shall not pass away,
and his kingdom one
that shall not be destroyed.[2]
(Daniel 7:9-10, 13b-14, RSV)

Jesus must have had this in mind when he promised his disciples that they would share in the judgment throne with the Son of Man:

Jesus said to them, "Truly I tell you, at the renewal of all things, when the Son of Man is seated on the throne of his glory, you who have followed me will also sit on twelve thrones, judging the twelve tribes of Israel." (Matthew 19:28, NRSV)

During his conversation with the disciples at the last supper, Jesus explicitly applied the role to himself:

"You are those who have continued with me in my trials; and I assign to you, as my Father assigned to me, a kingdom, that you may eat and drink at my table in my kingdom, and sit on thrones judging the twelve tribes of Israel. (Luke 22:28-30, NRSV)

Jesus is the Son of Man, the judge on that fearful day of the Lord. The possibility that the Son would occupy the judgment seat and render harsh verdict against the nations was a long-time hope of the people of God:

> I will tell of the decree of the Lord:
> He said to me, "You are my son;
>   today I have begotten you.
> Ask of me, and I will make the nations your
>   heritage,
>   and the ends of the earth your possession.
> You shall break them with a rod of iron,
>   and dash them in pieces like a potter's vessel."
> (Psalm 2:7-9, NRSV)

That is why it is so amazing that Jesus comes with words of blessing for the poor and lowly:

> Then he began to speak, and taught them, saying:
> "Blessed are the poor in spirit,
>   for theirs is the kingdom of heaven.
> "Blessed are those who mourn,
>   for they will be comforted.
> "Blessed are the meek,
>   for they will inherit the earth.
> "Blessed are those who hunger and thirst
>     for righteousness,
>   for they will be filled.
> "Blessed are the merciful,
>   for they will receive mercy.
> "Blessed are the pure in heart,
>   for they will see God."
> (Matthew 5:2-8, NRSV)

These blessings must not be read as words of instruction. They are declarations of the judgment of God on the humble of the earth, overturning all the unrighteous judgments of humankind. Here is the one who has been anointed to sit on the throne in judgment coming with the words of mercy promised by Jeremiah, "I will . . . remember their sin no more" (Jeremiah 31:34, NRSV).

The Gospel of John announces definitively:

> Indeed, God did not send the Son into the world
> to condemn the world, but in order that the world
> might be saved through him. (John 3:17, NRSV)

Forgiveness was Jesus' constant theme. He brought it to perfection on the cross when he prayed, "Father, forgive them; for they know not what they do" (Luke 23:34, RSV).

On the cross, Jesus absolutely and forever transformed judgment, infusing it with humility and grace. The judge of the world came and, instead of inflicting condemnation, he willingly chose the path of humility and suffering. Paul describes it this way:

> And being found in human form,
> he humbled himself
> and became obedient to the point of death—
> even death on a cross.
>
> Therefore God also highly exalted him
> and gave him the name
> that is above every name,
> so that at the name of Jesus
> every knee should bend,
> in heaven and on earth and under the earth. . . . [3]
> (Philippians 2:7b-10, NRSV)

As the Son of Man, and thus as God-appointed Judge of all humanity, Jesus voluntarily chose to suffer rather than inflict punishment. The Judge became the judged; the Lord, the servant. In this Jesus revealed the mercy which is, and has always been, at the heart of God.

### 'I will put my law within them.'

Having been freed from the burden of condemnation, the heart is free now to accept the gift of righteousness. It must have been infuriating to Paul that some would twist his teaching to imply that he believed that faith in God's grace meant that righteousness is not necessary for salvation. Twice, in Chapter 6 of his Letter to the Romans, he exclaims:

> What then are we to say? Should we continue in sin in order that grace may abound? By no means! (Romans 6:1, 15, NRSV)

The whole burden of Paul's Gospel (Romans 2:15-16; 16:25-26) is that in Christ he has found an answer to his life-long question: how can one obtain a genuine righteousness from God?

Paul wrestles with this theme in many of his letters. In his letters to the Corinthians (in which, by the way, Paul introduces the phrase "the new covenant" into the life of the church[4]), Paul argued vehemently that the community must show evidence of righteousness in their lives:

> Do you not know that wrongdoers will not inherit the kingdom of God? Do not be deceived! Fornicators, idolaters, adulterers, male prostitutes, sodomites, thieves, the greedy, drunkards, revilers, robbers—none of these will inherit the kingdom of God. And this is what some of you used to be. But you were washed, you were sanctified, you were justified in the name of the Lord Jesus Christ and in the Spirit of our God. . . .

> Or do you not know that your body is a temple of
> the Holy Spirit within you, which you have from
> God, and that you are not your own? For you were
> bought with a price; therefore glorify God in your
> body. (1 Corinthians 6:9-10, 19-20, NRSV)

Paul's fear is that—despite their confession that Jesus is Lord—
the Corinthians are defeating their salvation by wrongdoing.

Paul works out a theology of righteousness and grace in the
first eight chapters of his Letter to the Romans. He begins by
laying out his theme:

> For I am not ashamed of the gospel; it is the power
> of God for salvation to everyone who has faith, to
> the Jew first and also to the Greek. For in it the righ-
> teousness of God is revealed through faith for faith;
> as it is written, "The one who is righteous will live by
> faith." (Romans 1:17, NRSV)

Paul goes on to assert the necessity of right living for all
who would hope to be saved at the time of God's final judgment. After listing a catalogue of "every kind of evil" (from gos-
siping to greediness to murder), he writes:

> But by your hard and impenitent heart you are stor-
> ing up wrath for yourself on the day of wrath, when
> God's righteous judgment will be revealed. *For he
> will repay according to each one's deeds*: to those who
> by patiently doing good seek for glory and honor and
> immortality, he will give eternal life; while for those
> who are self-seeking and who obey not the truth but
> wickedness, there will be wrath and fury. There will
> be anguish and distress for everyone who does evil,
> the Jew first and also the Greek, but glory and honor
> and peace for everyone who does good, the Jew first
> and also the Greek. For God shows no partiality.
> (Romans 2:5-11, NRSV, my emphasis)

Those who misunderstand Paul to say that the only thing that matters for salvation is what one confesses with one's mouth (as an isolated reading of Romans 10:9 might imply) may have difficulty accepting his insistence that the basis of God's judgment will be one's deeds. However, in this he is consistent with the expectation of the prophets concerning the day of God's judgment.

Paul asserts that no one—neither Jews under the Law of God, nor Gentiles without the benefit of the Law—have achieved "goodness":

> as it is written: "There is no one who is righteous, not even one"; (Romans 3:10, NRSV)

In this, he is consistent with the realism of Jeremiah. Having detailed the dilemma, Paul looks to the death and resurrection of Jesus to find a solution:

> But now, apart from law, the righteousness of God has been disclosed, and is attested by the law and the prophets, the righteousness of God through faith in Jesus Christ for all who believe. For there is no distinction, since all have sinned and fall short of the glory of God; they are now justified by his grace as a gift, through the redemption that is in Christ Jesus, whom God put forward as a sacrifice of atonement by his blood, effective through faith. (Romans 3:21-25, NRSV)

Here, suddenly, Paul introduces the language of grace. The righteousness that is required by God comes from God as grace, i.e. as a gift. When accepted by faith, Christ's sacrificial death is our "justification" before God. Paul goes on to explain what this means.

Paul recalls the story of the Garden of Eden in order to explain that Christ's blood serves as an atonement for original sin. Paul calls Adam the first transgressor, "the pattern of the one to come" (Romans 5:14, NRSV). If Adam is the first transgressor, then Jesus is first restorer. Paul says:

> But the free gift is not like the trespass. For if the many died through the one man's trespass, much more surely have the grace of God and the free gift in the grace of the one man, Jesus Christ, abounded for the many. (Romans 5:15, NRSV)

Paul recalls the source of sin (symbolically expressed in Adam and Eve's act of eating the fruit of the tree of the knowledge of good and evil) and asserts that God has found a way to free humanity from it. In Jesus, our alienation from God because of the human desire to make independent judgment of good and evil is being overcome.

For Paul, Adam's sin and Christ's atonement are not only external and objective facts. Paul shows how they become internal realities when he turns next to the subject of baptism. Paul characterizes baptism in Christ as a "baptism into death" (Romans 6:4, NRSV). For Paul, the baptism that brings us into salvation goes far beyond the ritual of water baptism. Paul insists that an effective baptism involves a spiritual dynamic deep within the believer:

> The death he [i.e., Jesus] died, he died to sin, once for all; but the life he lives, he lives to God. So you also must consider yourselves dead to sin and alive to God in Christ Jesus. Therefore, do not let sin exercise dominion in your mortal bodies, to make you obey their passions. No longer present your members to sin as instruments of wickedness, but present

yourselves to God as those who have been brought from death to life, and present your members to God as instruments of righteousness. (Romans 6:10-13, NRSV)

This is the turning point in Paul's argument. Paul is here talking about the spiritual dynamic of bringing the individual will into a condition of yieldedness to God. The only adequate language for this transaction is death: death to that willfulness that had been seeking to make judgments of good and evil independently of God. This death is good news because it is the only way to a life that actually experiences the righteousness of God:

But thanks be to God that you, having once been slaves of sin, have become *obedient from the heart* to the form of teaching to which you were entrusted, and that you, having been set free from sin, have become slaves of righteousness. (Romans 6:17-18, NRSV, my emphasis)

In the next two chapters of Romans, Paul contrasts the Law of Moses with the Law of the Spirit. The climax of Paul's teaching comes in Chapter 8:

For the law of the Spirit of life in Christ Jesus has set you free from the law of sin and of death. For God has done what the law, weakened by the flesh, could not do: by sending his own Son in the likeness of sinful flesh, and to deal with sin, he condemned sin in the flesh, so that the just requirement of the law might be fulfilled in us, who walk not according to the flesh but according to the Spirit.

For those who live according to the flesh set their minds on the things of the flesh, but those who live according to the Spirit set their minds on the things of the Spirit. To set the mind on the flesh is death, but to set the mind on the Spirit is life and peace. For this reason the mind that is set on the flesh is hostile to God; it does not submit to God's law—indeed it cannot, and those who are in the flesh cannot please God.

But you are not in the flesh; you are in the Spirit, since the Spirit of God dwells in you. Anyone who does not have the Spirit of Christ does not belong to him. But if Christ is in you, though the body is dead because of sin, the Spirit is life because of righteousness. (Romans 8:2-10, NRSV)

The Law of Moses and the Law of the Spirit both flow from God. They both reflect the will of God. They both reflect God's intentions from the beginning for the happiness of all the creation. The Law of the Spirit, however, is essentially different from the Law of Moses in that it reaches beyond the deceiving power of the intellect to change the heart and life of the believer. In fact, the Law of the Spirit does not function externally to the individual at all. It is inward, a function of the inherence of Christ, born in the believer through faith.

Elsewhere, Paul summarized all of this in the phrase, "Christ in you, the hope of glory" (Colossians 1:27b, NRSV). The righteousness that God demands is itself a gift of God alone: it is the fruit of an inward transformation of the heart and mind through the gift of the Holy Spirit who writes the law of God on the hearts of believers. It is the gift of a heart of flesh.

*'They will all know me.'*

At the heart of the new covenant is the promise that everyone can have a personal, inward knowledge of God:

> No longer shall they teach one another, or say to each other, "Know the Lord," for they shall all know me, from the least of them to the greatest, says the Lord. (Jeremiah 31:34a, NRSV)

This intimacy with God will be so great that there will be no need for external, human instruction. John connected the anointing of the Holy Spirit and this new covenant promise when he wrote, "As for you, the anointing that you received from him abides in you, and so you do not need anyone to teach you" (1 John 2:27a, NRSV). This promise was fulfilled on the day of Pentecost.

On the day of Pentecost, the outpouring of the Holy Spirit on the disciples was so overwhelming that bystanders first assumed that the disciples were drunk. Peter tried to explain what had happened:

> No, this is what was spoken through the prophet Joel:
> 'In the last days it will be, God declares,
>   that I will pour out my Spirit upon all flesh,
>     and your sons and your daughters shall prophesy,
>     and your young men shall see visions,
>     and your old men shall dream dreams.
> Even upon my slaves, both men and women,
>   in those days I will pour out my Spirit;
>     and they shall prophesy.
> And I will show portents in the heaven above
>   and signs on the earth below,
>     blood, and fire, and smoky mist.

> The sun shall be turned to darkness
>  and the moon to blood,
>  before the coming of the Lord's great and glorious
>  day.
> Then everyone who calls on the name of the Lord
>  shall be saved.'
>
> (Acts 2:17-21, NRSV)

In these last days,[5] everyone regardless of class or condition of life gets to "know" God dwelling with them. The promise, "they shall all know me, from the least to the greatest," is fulfilled by the gifts of the Holy Spirit, and even more by the continuing presence of the Holy Spirit as teacher.

There are two gifts of the Spirit that are particularly concerned with the direct communication between God and people. Paul writes about this in his letters to the church in Corinth. One is the gift of tongues, the other is prophecy. Paul understands the gift of tongues to be a prayer language through which believers praise God and commune inwardly with God. The devious intellect, which is prone to rationalize our own desires, is by-passed so that God and the believer speak directly, heart-to-heart. Paul is adamant that this is a good thing, and even boasts, "I thank God that I speak in tongues more than all of you" (1 Corinthians 14:18, NRSV).

As good as the gift of tongues is, Paul's major concern is that the word of God should be heard by everyone, so he urges the priority of the gift of prophecy:

> Pursue love and strive for the spiritual gifts, and especially that you may prophesy. For those who speak in a tongue do not speak to other people but to God; for nobody understands them, since they are speaking mysteries in the Spirit.

> On the other hand, those who prophesy speak to
> other people for their upbuilding and encourage-
> ment and consolation. Those who speak in a tongue
> build up themselves, but those who prophesy build
> up the church. Now I would like all of you to speak
> in tongues, but even more to prophesy. One who
> prophesies is greater than one who speaks in tongues,
> unless someone interprets, so that the church may
> be built up. (1 Corinthians 14:1-5, NRSV)

Prophecy is the gift of uttering whatever words God wants people to hear at that specific time and place. Paul is careful to explain that prophecy includes words of comfort or encour-agement, direction and wisdom. It is not confined to foretell-ing the future, or to criticism of people or society for their lack of justice—though God, of course, often inspires prophets to say things of that sort. What makes prophecy authentic is that the words, whatever they may be, originate in the Spirit of God and reflect direct communication from God, who is the Word.

The promise that "all will know me, from the least to the greatest" (Jeremiah 31:34, NRSV) is fulfilled through the gifts of tongues and prophecy but, most of all, it is fulfilled through the gift of the Counselor that Jesus promised in the Gospel of John. According to that Gospel, during the last sup-per, Jesus accepted the designation, "Teacher and Lord" (John 13:13). Following the meal, Jesus gave a long discourse about how this relationship could continue and even grow because his coming death would enable believers to enjoy the gift of the Holy Spirit:

> And I will ask the Father, and he will give you an-
> other Counselor to be with you forever—the Spirit
> of truth. The world cannot accept him, because it

neither sees him nor knows him. But you know him, for he lives with you and will be in you.

I will not leave you as orphans; I will come to you. Before long, the world will not see me anymore, but you will see me. Because I live, you also will live. On that day you will realize that I am in my Father, and you are in me, and I am in you. . . .

All this I have spoken while still with you. But the Counselor, the Holy Spirit, whom the Father will send in my name, will teach you all things and will remind you of everything I have said to you. (John 14:16-20, 25-26, NIV)

Because the resurrected Jesus dwells both with God and, through the Holy Spirit, within the believer, it is possible for the believer to live by the living words of the living God.

This is the linchpin of salvation. According to Jesus, eternal life starts in this life and depends on attending to the living word of God:

"Very truly, I tell you, anyone who hears my word and believes him who sent me has eternal life, and does not come under judgment, but has passed from death to life." (John 5:24, NRSV)

Jesus is scornful of those who would substitute the written record of God's voice in scripture for the contemporary experience of the living voice of God:

"And the Father who sent me has himself testified on my behalf. You have never heard his voice or seen his form, and you do not have his word abiding in you, because you do not believe him whom he has sent.

"You search the scriptures because you think that in them you have eternal life; and it is they that testify on my behalf. Yet you refuse to come to me to have life." (John 5:37-40, NRSV)

Life is in the *qol Yahweh*, the living voice of God, not in the record of it. Of course, this implies no rejection of the scriptures. Rather, Jesus insists that the authoritative words of scripture point to the living relationship between humanity and God that is being restored by him through the gift of the Holy Spirit.

James, the brother of Jesus and the leader of the post-resurrection church in Jerusalem, brings together the themes of righteousness, salvation, and the inward experience of the living word of God:

Therefore rid yourselves of all sordidness and rank growth of wickedness, and welcome with meekness *the implanted word* [my emphasis] that has the power to save your souls. (James 1:21, NRSV)

This implanted word opens the door to the kingdom of heaven. The word, implanted by the Holy Spirit, brings true righteousness into our lives so that we are, in reality, fit to stand before God on the day of judgment. It is therefore possible to say that this implanted word has the power to save. James' "implanted word," John's "Counselor," and Paul's "law of the Spirit" are one and the same: the gift of God's continuing presence as inward teacher by which God gives and continually renews a heart of flesh in the believer.

Isaiah foresaw the joy that would come to those who received the righteousness of God in their hearts; it would be as if the barrenness of exile had become the paradise of God:

> For the Lord will comfort Zion; he will comfort all
> her waste places, and will make her wilderness like
> Eden, her desert like the garden of the Lord; joy and
> gladness will be found in her, thanksgiving and the
> voice of song.
>
> Listen to me, my people, and give heed to me, my
> nation; for a teaching will go out from me, and my
> justice for a light to the peoples. . . . *Listen to me,*
> *you who know righteousness, you people who have my*
> *teaching in your hearts.* . . . (Isaiah 51:3-4, 7a, NRSV,
> my emphasis)

### Salvation in This World and the Next

Jesus made the extraordinary claim that eternal life begins
in this life whenever a believer attends to the living voice of
God; it extends into eternity. The Book of Revelation offers
this vision of that life:

> And I heard a loud voice from the throne saying,
> "See, the home of God is among mortals. He will
> dwell with them; they will be his peoples, and God
> himself will be with them; he will wipe every tear
> from their eyes. Death will be no more; mourning
> and crying and pain will be no more, for the first
> things have passed away."
>
> And the one who was seated on the throne said,
> "See, I am making all things new." (Revelation 21:3-
> 5, NRSV)

This vision is an image of the resurrection life that Enoch and
the Maccabees believed was only possible in a future beyond
the final judgment. When Jesus announced that the "kingdom
of God" is "at hand" (Mark 1:15; Matthew 3:2 4:17; 10:7; Luke

10:9) he proclaimed that, in him, people could experience the power of the resurrection, now.

Jesus' miraculous healings manifest the inbreaking of the resurrection life where "crying and pain will be no more." It is for this reason that Jesus often employed the language of salvation when he healed:

> Now there was a woman who had been suffering from hemorrhages for twelve years. She had endured much under many physicians, and had spent all that she had; and she was no better, but rather grew worse. She had heard about Jesus, and came up behind him in the crowd and touched his cloak, for she said, "If I but touch his clothes, I will be made well." Immediately her hemorrhage stopped; and she felt in her body that she was healed of her disease.
>
> Immediately aware that power had gone forth from him, Jesus turned about in the crowd and said, "Who touched my clothes?" And his disciples said to him, "You see the crowd pressing in on you; how can you say, 'Who touched me?'" He looked all around to see who had done it.
>
> But the woman, knowing what had happened to her, came in fear and trembling, fell down before him, and told him the whole truth. He said to her, "Daughter, your faith has made you well; go in peace, and be healed of your disease." (Mark 5:25-34, NRSV)

In this translation, Jesus' words, "your faith has made you well," paraphrase the Greek words that literally read, "your faith has saved/*sesoken* you."[6] It is unfortunate that this is obscured, because the use of the language of salvation is chosen in intentional parallelism with the following phrase, "go in peace, and be healed of your disease," where Jesus uses a term for physical healing or wholeness. By putting the two together, Jesus makes clear that restored health was a manifestation of this woman's salvation. The kingdom of God was at hand.

Nearly half the occasions when scripture records Jesus using the language of salvation, he is speaking about miracles of healing. In Luke 17:11-19, for example, when the ten lepers are healed but only one returns to give thanks, Jesus says: "your faith has made you well" (Luke 17:19, NRSV). Again, the Greek literally reads, "your faith has saved/*sesoken* you."

In this life, the reality is that crying and pain and death continue. But miraculously, the faithful discover that God is with them wiping the tears from their eyes, and, from time to time, God graciously restores health to bodies as a foretaste of the resurrection to come. Jesus commissioned his twelve disciples, and then seventy others, to carry this saving power out into the world:

> Then Jesus summoned his twelve disciples and gave them authority over unclean spirits, to cast them out, and to cure every disease and every sickness. . . . "As you go, proclaim the good news, 'The kingdom of heaven has come near.' Cure the sick, raise the dead, cleanse the lepers, cast out demons." (Matthew 10:1, 7-8a, NRSV; Luke 10:1, 8-9)

Praying for healing is integral to the proclamation of salvation. After Pentecost, when Peter and John entered the Temple court to pray, a crippled beggar accosted them, asking for money. Peter looked at him and said,

> "I have no silver or gold, but what I have I give you; in the name of Jesus Christ of Nazareth, stand up and walk." (Acts 3:6, NRSV)

The beggar was instantly healed, and famously went away jumping and leaping in his joy. The astonishment of the people was the occasion of Peter's most profound sermon about salvation:

> "You Israelites, why do you wonder at this, or why do you stare at us, as though by our own power or piety we had made him walk? The God of Abraham, the God of Isaac, and the God of Jacob, the God of our ancestors has glorified his servant Jesus, whom you handed over and rejected. . . . And by faith in his name, his name itself has made this man strong, whom you see and know; and the faith that is through Jesus has given him this perfect health in the presence of all of you.
>
> "And now, friends, I know that you acted in ignorance, as did also your rulers. In this way God fulfilled what he had foretold through all the prophets, that his Messiah would suffer. Repent therefore, and turn to God so that your sins may be wiped out, so that times of refreshing may come from the presence of the Lord, and that he may send the Messiah appointed for you, that is, Jesus, who must remain in heaven until the time of universal restoration that God announced long ago through his holy prophets.
>
> "Moses said, 'The Lord your God will raise up for you from your own people a prophet like me. You must listen to whatever he tells you. And it will be that everyone who does not listen to that prophet will be utterly rooted out of the people.'" (Acts 3:12-13, 16-23, NRSV, referencing Deuteronomy 15:15, 19)

Thus, Peter ties together (1) healing by faith in Jesus' name, with (2) the cross and forgiveness of sins, (3) the identification of Jesus with the prophet to whom "you must listen," and (4) "universal restoration." This is the core of salvation through faith: That in the course of listening to Jesus the Messianic prophet—who is now available to us as our Counselor through the Holy Spirit—God restores to us the blessings of paradise that were known at the beginning of creation. Now we enjoy, in part, a foretaste of this restoration. We perceive that these "times of refreshing" are merely a down payment on the universal restoration of paradise that we will ultimately experience in fullness in the general resurrection to come.

Paul also wrote about this "down payment":

> It is God who establishes us with you in Christ and has anointed us, by putting his seal on us and giving us his Spirit in our hearts as a first installment. (2 Corinthians 1:21-22, NRSV)

> But we must always give thanks to God for you, brothers and sisters beloved by the Lord, because God chose you as the first fruits for salvation through sanctification by the Spirit and through belief in the truth. (2 Thessalonians 2:13, NRSV)

As we eagerly await the restoration of all things, we receive the down payment of the Holy Spirit bearing the fruit of the tree of life in our lives:

> the fruit of the Spirit is love, joy, peace, patience, kindness, generosity, faithfulness, gentleness, and self-control. (Galatians 5:22-23a, NRSV)

These qualities have the fragrance of Eden. Our lives become more like Christ's; they become signs of salvation.

<sup></sup>[1] This point provides an important theological basis for the rejection of Constantinian Christianity and political Zionism. Salvation in the new covenant is incompatible with a state church.

[2] This understanding of the "Son of Man" was current in Jewish thought in the years prior to Jesus. Compare this passage from 1 Enoch:

"(Then) there came to them a great joy. And they blessed, glorified, and extolled (the Lord) [because] the name of that (Son of) Man was revealed to them. He shall never pass away or perish from before the face of the earth. But those who have led the world astray shall be bound with chains; and their ruinous congregation shall be imprisoned; all their deeds shall vanish from before the face of the earth. Thenceforth nothing that is corruptible shall be found; for that Son of Man has appeared and has seated himself upon the throne of his glory; and all evil shall disappear from before his face; he shall go and tell to that Son of Man, and he shall be strong before the LORD of the Spirits." (1 Enoch 69:27-29) Charlesworth, *The Old Testament Pseudepigrapha*, Vol. 1, (Garden City, NY: Doubleday Company, Inc., 1985) 49.

[3] This early hymn of the church alludes to, but changes, God's words from Isaiah 45:22-23 (NRSV):

Turn to me and be saved, all you ends of the earth;
  for I am God, and there is no other.
By myself I have sworn,
  my mouth has uttered in all integrity a word that will not
    be revoked:
Before me every knee *will* bow;
  by me every tongue *will* swear.

Here God affirms his future victory in power—"every knee will bow"—but the Christian hymn transforms the future tense "will" into the subjunctive, "should" underlining the awe with which they acknowledged God's self-emptying sacrifice in taking on human limitation and suffering. Here, indeed is something at which every knee *should* bow! God's triumph comes not in power but through humility.

[4] The term, "new covenant," appears in the New Testament only in Paul's Corinthian correspondence [1 Corinthians 11:25; 2 Corinthians 3:6], the Gospel of Luke, and the Letter to the Hebrews. Both of the latter are dependent on Paul or his disciples and are later than the Corinthian letters.

[5] Speculation about whether we are approaching the "end times" is fruitless—not least because the scripture is clear that Pentecost inaugurated the "last days." Who are we to judge how many of our 24-hour days we will experience before God brings the last days to their end?

[6] This association of salvation and restoration of health would not have surprised early Christians. It was, for instance, similar to the language they would have found in Psalm 30:

O Lord, you brought up my soul from Sheol,
    restored me to life from among those gone down to the Pit.
                                (Psalm 30:3, NRSV)

Where the Hebrew reads, "you . . . restored me to life," the Septuagint (the Greek translation of the Hebrew scriptures current in Jesus' time) has, "you . . . saved/*esosas* me from among those going down into the pit."

# THE SIGN OF THE
# LISTENING COMMUNITY

*J*esus' call always comes to individuals and places them in community. We are saved into community. The story of salvation has been the story of God gathering and preserving a people: from the time when God promised Abraham and Sarah that through their descendents "all the families on earth shall be blessed" (Genesis 12:3, NRSV); through the miraculous deliverance of that family from famine; through Joseph's captivity and rise to power in Egypt; through the mass exodus from Egypt and the deliverance of the people from Pharaoh's army at the Red Sea; through the deliverances of the judges from the oppression of the Philistines and other enemies, and on through the prophets and kings.

> For you are a people holy to the Lord your God; the Lord your God has chosen you out of all the peoples on earth to be his people, his treasured possession. It was not because you were more numerous than any other people that the Lord set his heart on you and chose you—for you were the fewest of all peoples. It was because the Lord loved you. . . . (Deuteronomy 7:6-8a, NRSV)

Here is both the greatness and the weakness of God, that God has chosen to love. It is greatness because, by making the

choice of love, God has given meaning to the universe and purpose to life; it is weakness because a lover cannot force responsive love, but only woo it. Genuine love is the guarantor of
the freedom of the beloved; when God chose love, God chose
to limit his own power. It may be said that human freedom
to rebel against God is the direct measure of God's love for
humanity.

God is under no compulsion to love humankind, but, despite heartbreak and disappointment, God returns to the ob-
jects of his first love, and "remembers his covenant." (Leviticus
26:42ff; Ezekiel 16:60-61; Luke 1:72) God's greatest desire is
to have fellowship with the people whom he loves:

> And I will walk among you, and will be your God,
> and you shall be my people. (Leviticus 26:12, NRSV;
> cf., Exodus 6:7)

Here, at the climax of the decrees of the law, are echoes of
Eden, where the Lord walked in the garden with Adam and
Eve at the time of the moving of the spirit. Here is yearning
for reciprocated love that reaches back into the mystery of creation and offers an answer to the ultimate question, "Why?"
God created *because* God wants to be with us: Immanuel. Yet,
humankind has not reciprocated God's love.

Humanity continually chooses to reject God, who is the
very basis of its freedom:

> But this command I gave them, "Obey my voice/*qol*,
> and I will be your God, and you shall be my people;
> and walk only in the way that I command you, so
> that it may be well with you."
>
> Yet they did not obey or incline their ear, but, in the
> stubbornness of their evil will, they walked in their
> own counsels.... (Jeremiah 7:23-24b, NRSV)

When God says, "Obey," it is not the edict of a tyrant but the longing of the One who is love (1 John 4:8, 16) to provide for the welfare of the people whom he loves. By their stubborn rejection of the *qol Yahweh*, the people of God destroy their unity with God and with one another. Here is the root of all injustice and hatred: rejection of the love that resides at the heart of the universe. It is to repair the covenant of love ("a covenant that they broke, though I was their husband") (Jeremiah 31:32, NRSV), and to reinstate humanity in a freedom that is free from injustice and hatred, that God in Christ inaugurated the new covenant.

Jesus' work is to recreate in us, on the basis of a personal and inward knowledge of God, the outward community of those called to be the people of God. Jesus speaks of his yearning to gather people together, "How often have I desired to gather your children together as a hen gathers her brood under her wings" (Matthew 23:37, NRSV). When he sent out his disciples and apostles (Matthew 10; Luke 9:1-5, 10:1-16), he did not commission them to call for individual professions of faith, but rather to announce that "the kingdom of God is at hand." It is no accident that Jesus used the social term "kingdom." Salvation, inevitably, is a communal enterprise.

When Jesus taught us prayer, we did not learn, "My father," but, "Our Father. . . . " When Jesus told of the shepherd who had a hundred sheep but lost one and left the ninety-nine to find the one who was lost, the force of the parable concerned God's desire to restore the wholeness of the community.[1] God, he is saying, would rather risk the whole enterprise of salvation than allow the community of the saved to be diminished by even one. The measure of the strength of community is not the health of the strongest but of the weakest.

Jesus carried this emphasis on community into his ministry of healing and restoration. Although healing touches the life and body of specific individuals, Jesus not only delivers the individual sufferer but restores the community of God's people. Jesus' ministry to the widow of Nain, whose son he raised from the dead, offers a good example:

> Soon afterwards he went to a town called Nain, and his disciples and a large crowd went with him. As he approached the gate of the town, a man who had died was being carried out. He was his mother's only son, and she was a widow; and with her was a large crowd from the town. When the Lord saw her, he had compassion for her and said to her, "Do not weep." Then he came forward and touched the bier, and the bearers stood still. And he said, "Young man, I say to you, rise!" The dead man sat up and began to speak, and Jesus gave him to his mother.
>
> Fear seized all of them; and they glorified God, saying, "A great prophet has risen among us!" and "God has looked favorably on his people!" (Luke 7:11-16, NRSV)

When God comforts one, it is a sign of God's compassion for the whole community, as the people of Nain themselves testified.

The emphasis on community is not on Jesus' lips alone; it infuses all strands of the New Testament. In the Letter to Hebrews, after the long discourse on Jesus as the High Priest and mediator of the new covenant, comes this exhortation:

> And let us consider how to provoke one another to love and good deeds, not neglecting to meet together, as is the habit of some, but encouraging one another,

and all the more as you see the Day approaching.
(Hebrews 10:24-25, NRSV)

If we neglect the assembly, we neglect our salvation, because, as
the author of Hebrews says, we are all in this together:

> But you have come to Mount Zion and to the city
> of the living God, the heavenly Jerusalem, and to in-
> numerable angels in festal gathering, and to the as-
> sembly of the firstborn who are enrolled in heaven,
> and to God the judge of all, and to the spirits of the
> righteous made perfect, and to Jesus, the mediator
> of a new covenant, and to the sprinkled blood that
> speaks a better word than the blood of Abel. See
> that you do not refuse the one who is speaking . . . !
> (Hebrews 12:22-25a, NRSV)

The life of the community gathered by the living word of
God—that innumerable assembly of angels and believers that
extends across time as well as space (Hebrews 11)—is the sign
of the kingdom of God.

Not only is it impossible to be saved in isolation because our
salvation is into the community of God's chosen, it is impossible to evangelize without the living evidence provided by the
community of faith. Speaking to his disciples, Jesus says, "You
[plural] are the light of the world. A city built on a hill cannot
be hid" (Matthew 5:14, NRSV). Similarly, Peter writes:

> But you are a chosen race, a royal priesthood, a holy
> nation, God's own people, *in order that you may pro-
> claim* the mighty acts of him who called you out of
> darkness into his marvelous light. Once you were
> not a people, but now you are God's people; once you
> had not received mercy, but now you have received
> mercy. (1 Peter 2:9-10, NRSV, my emphasis)

Either our lives carry the smell and light of Eden, or they do not. Either our lives demonstrate that we are saved from the first "not good" of loneliness into loving fellowship, or not. Either our lives reflect the peace and abundance of Eden, or not. None of this can be demonstrated in an isolated life; these signs can only be lived in community.

Individual lives may be winsome and testify to God's love, but they only become truly invitational as part of the life of a community that demonstrates it has been transformed by the presence of the voice of God walking in its midst." We are saved *through* community and *into* community.

### The Mystery of Inclusion

The problem with community is that, all too often, it defines itself by walls of exclusivity. Within those walls the community is loving; but outsiders know that they are indeed outside. There is a false corollary to the idea of being "a chosen people," namely that everyone else has *not* been chosen: if God loves me, then God does not love you.

This, Jesus excoriates. Jesus calls himself the Good Shepherd, and says the basis of the community of faith is that the sheep recognize and follow his voice:

> The gatekeeper opens the gate for him, and the sheep hear his voice. He calls his own sheep by name and leads them out. When he has brought out all his own, he goes ahead of them, and the sheep follow him because they know his voice. . . .
>
> I am the good shepherd. I know my own and my own know me, just as the Father knows me and I know the Father. And I lay down my life for the sheep. (John 10:3-4, 14, NRSV)

Then, he immediately surprises us with the good news that there are "other sheep" in other flocks who are also his:

> I have other sheep that do not belong to this fold. I must bring them also, and they will listen to my voice. So there will be one flock, one shepherd. (John 10:16, NRSV)

If salvation is a safe and abundant pasture, we enter it as members of a flock. Rubbing shoulders, learning to share, learning to love, we are saved together by just one thing: listening to the voice of the shepherd. Along the way, we discover the extraordinary truth that our flock is not the whole story; others whom we would never have recognized before have also responded to the voice of the shepherd we love.[2] What a shock! What a joy!

Jesus was willing to give his life for this principle. According to the Gospel of Luke, Jesus gave an inaugural sermon in his home town of Nazareth in which he set out the great themes of his ministry. He first announced the year of God's favor. At this, "all bore witness to Him, and marveled at the gracious words" (Luke 4:22, NKJ), and no wonder: he was announcing that the liberating power of God's love was being unleashed in their midst. Then he went on to talk about the universality of the love of God as it extended beyond the ethnic composition of their community and the political boundaries of Israel. This shattered his home-folk's understanding of themselves as the exclusively chosen. For this he was nearly killed. Here is what Jesus said, and what happened next:

> "But the truth is, there were many widows in Israel in the time of Elijah, when the heaven was shut up three years and six months, and there was a severe famine over all the land; yet Elijah was sent to none

of them except to a widow at Zarephath in [the Phoenician town of] Sidon. There were also many lepers in Israel in the time of the prophet Elisha, and none of them was cleansed except Naaman the Syrian."

When they heard this, all in the synagogue were filled with rage. They got up, drove him out of the town, and led him to the brow of the hill on which their town was built, so that they might hurl him off the cliff. (Luke 4:25-30, NRSV)

So, at the beginning of his ministry, Jesus risked everything to explode the boundaries of God's chosen people.

No one understood the significance of this more clearly than the Apostle Paul. The inclusiveness of the Gospel became linchpin of his ministry. In his Letter to the Ephesians, he called it "the mystery of Christ," and proclaimed:

Although I am the very least of all the saints, this grace was given to me to bring to the Gentiles the news of *the boundless riches of Christ*, and to make everyone see what is the plan of the mystery hidden for ages in God who created all things; his intent was that now, *through the church, the manifold wisdom of God* should be made known to the rulers and authorities in the heavenly realms, according to his eternal purpose which he accomplished in Christ Jesus our Lord. (Ephesians 3:8-11, NIV, my emphasis)

The mystery to be "made known" through the life of the church is that Christ, through the cross, has broken down the walls of exclusivity that had appeared to limit the designation "chosen people" to the descendents of Abraham and Sarah. Paul, reminding the Gentiles of the requirement of circumcision in the Abrahamic covenant, explained:

So then, remember that at one time you Gentiles by birth, called "the uncircumcision" by those who are called "the circumcision"—a physical circumcision made in the flesh by human hands—remember that you were at that time without Christ, being aliens from the commonwealth of Israel, and strangers to the covenants of promise, having no hope and without God in the world.

But now in Christ Jesus you who once were far off have been brought near by the blood of Christ. For he is our peace; in his flesh he has made both groups into one and has broken down the dividing wall, that is, the hostility between us. He has abolished the law with its commandments and ordinances, *that he might create in himself one new humanity* in place of the two, thus making peace, and might reconcile both groups to God in one body through the cross, thus putting to death that hostility through it. So he came and proclaimed peace to you who were far off and peace to those who were near; for through him both of us have access in one Spirit to the Father.

So then you are no longer strangers and aliens, but you are citizens with the saints and also members of the household of God, built upon the foundation of the apostles and prophets, with Christ Jesus himself as the cornerstone. In him the whole structure is joined together and grows into a holy temple in the Lord; in whom you also are built together spiritually into a dwelling place for God. (Ephesians 2:11-22, NRSV, my emphasis)

From this flows all that Paul taught about inclusion, love, and equality within the church. Were the circumcised and the uncircumcised to be equal in the church? This question came to a head in a debate about "table fellowship" between those who did and those who did not follow the Mosaic laws regarding clean and unclean foods. Paul concludes:

> God made you alive together with him, when he forgave us all our trespasses, erasing the record that stood against us with its legal demands. He set this aside, nailing it to the cross. . . . Therefore do not let anyone condemn you in matters of food and drink. . . . (Colossians 2:13b-14, 16a, NRSV)

When he saw Peter back away from the principle of full equality between Jew and Gentile, Paul wrote that even though Peter was the chief apostle, "I opposed him to his face" (Galatians 2:11, NRSV). The inclusiveness of the Gospel was at stake.

Was there a question about the full partnership of slaves in the community of salvation? This is the subject of the Letter to Philemon. Philemon's slave Onesimus had run away and found Paul, who was then in captivity in Rome. Paul sent him back to Philemon (Onesimus' putative owner) but with the strenuous insistence that the relationship must be transformed:

> Perhaps this is the reason he was separated from you for a while, so that you might have him back forever, no longer as a slave but more than a slave, a beloved brother—especially to me but how much more to you, both in the flesh and in the Lord. (Philemon 15-16, NRSV)

With the expression "both in the flesh and in the Lord," Paul underlines his expectation that the relationship between Philemon and Onesimus is to be transformed in practical ways, and not just spiritually. Jesus had announced that his ministry would reveal the "acceptable year of the Lord," and it is intriguing to think that when Paul demanded that Onesimus be set free, this fulfilled one of the requirements of the acceptable year (See Deuteronomy 15:12-17).

What was at issue was not Onesimus' obedience, or Philemon's rights, but the wholeness of the community. Paul begins his letter to Philemon by praying, "that the fellowship/*koinonia* of your faith may become effective through the knowledge of every good thing which is in you for Christ's sake" (Philemon 6, NAS). Equality within the church restores the fellowship, and that is key to the blessings Christ has for us as individuals.

What about social class distinctions? They were eliminated. Paul was scathing in his attack on the Corinthian church for the way its members had treated the poor during the Lord's supper. The supper was celebrated in the form of a carry-in feast, and, while some gorged, those without wealth looked hungrily on:

> Or do you show contempt for the church of God and humiliate those who have nothing? What should I say to you? Should I commend you? In this matter I do not commend you! (1 Corinthians 11:22b; see also James 2:1-6, NRSV)

Paul goes on to say,

> Whoever, therefore, eats the bread or drinks the cup of the Lord in an unworthy manner will be answerable for the body and blood of the Lord. (1 Corinthians 11:27, NRSV)

When the poor have been discriminated against, the body and blood of Christ have been desecrated because the fellowship of the church is the living body of the Lord (See, 1 Corinthians 12:27).

Was there a dispute about whether women have a full place in the life of the fellowship? Paul writes to the Corinthians about women's ministry in the church in the matter of prophesying (i.e., the authoritative preaching of the living word) and public prayer. For Paul it is obvious. Of course women are to pray and preach in the church! (1 Corinthians 11:5)[3] "But all things should be done decently and in order" (1 Corinthians 14:40, NRSV). After acknowledging the importance of conforming to social customs regarding head coverings, Paul lays down the rule of the equality and mutual dependence of the sexes under God:

> Nevertheless, in the Lord woman is not independent of man or man independent of woman. For just as woman came from man, so man comes through woman; but all things come from God. (1 Corinthians 11:11-12, NRSV)

For Paul, all of this is a necessary corollary to the mystery of the cross: that the barriers of separation have been torn down by the blood of Christ. He sums it up in his letter to the Galatians:

> in Christ Jesus you are all children of God through faith. . . . There is no longer Jew or Greek, there is no longer slave or free, there is no longer male and female; for all of you are one in Christ Jesus. And if you belong to Christ, then you are Abraham's offspring, heirs according to the promise. (Galatians 3:26, 28-29, NRSV)

It is the destiny of the church (i.e., the assembly of God's people) to demonstrate the inclusiveness of God's love. God has chosen a people to love, and no one shall be excluded from that company! A divided church, an exclusive church, a restricted church, is a negation of the cross and the denial of God's saving work. Only an inclusive church reflects God's promise in the new covenant that "all will know me from the least to the greatest" (Jeremiah 31:34a, NRSV).

### The Countersign of Mutual Submission

How will the inclusive community retain its unity as a people bound together by the voice of the Shepherd, as each member attends to the law written on his or her heart? How will the inclusive community give witness to the righteousness that comes from God alone, as believers from every background express truth in ways that make sense in their very different cultural contexts? The new covenant community finds the answer to these questions in the presence of Christ as teacher and head of the church through the distribution of the gifts of the Holy Spirit, and in a system of discipline based upon the principle of mutual submission under God.

A community that takes seriously the universal pouring out of the Spirit at Pentecost requires forms of community life and governance that are radically different from any known before. The promise is that

> your sons and your daughters shall prophesy,
>   and your young men shall see visions,
>   and your old men shall dream dreams.
> Even upon my slaves, both men and women,
>   in those days I will pour out my Spirit;
>   and they shall prophesy.
>     (Acts 2:17b-18, NRSV; cf., Joel 2:28-29)

What if slaves were excluded or women subordinated or children despised or the elderly ignored or the poor turned away?

What if all were "welcomed" but some prohibited from speaking? The consequence would be that the community of God's people could not hear the words God was delivering through them; God's direct rule over the community would thereby be diminished; the kingdom of God would be overthrown. Therefore, the community of God's people must find a way to hear the word of God potentially expressed by *anyone*.

This was foreshadowed in the earlier history of salvation. Moses gathered seventy elders to help him in his work. God took some of the Spirit that had been resting on Moses and anointed the seventy elders, "and when the spirit rested upon them, they prophesied. But they did not do so again" (Numbers 11:25, NRSV). Two others, Eldad and Medad, however, also received the Spirit and apparently they kept on prophesying.

> And a young man ran and told Moses, "Eldad and Medad are prophesying in the camp." And Joshua son of Nun, the assistant of Moses, one of his chosen men, said, "My lord Moses, stop them!"
>
> But Moses said to him, "Are you jealous for my sake? Would that all the Lord's people were prophets, and that the Lord would put his spirit on them!" (Numbers 11:27-29, NRSV)

In the generations after Moses, the system of rule over the tribes of Israel had been decentralized and charismatic. Judges were raised up by God and anointed to "deliver" the people at times of need. The judges were male and female, drawn from many different tribes and families. But, at the time when Samuel was judge over Israel, the people envied the apparent stability of other nations and clamored for a king. God (cherishing the freedom of his people) agreed to their demands, but saw this centralization of power in human dynasties as a repudiation of "the kingdom of God":

> and the Lord said to Samuel, "Listen to the voice of the people in all that they say to you; for they have not rejected you, but they have rejected me from being king over them." (1 Samuel 8:7, NRSV)

The prophets continued to serve as a check and rebuke to the power of the kings of Israel. But it was only with Jesus' proclamation of the kingdom of God "at hand" that the direct rule of God over the people of God was restored.

The first step in restoring the immediate rule of God is to dethrone all other pretenders to the crown. Jesus was quick to do this in the circle of his disciples. Catching them in an argument about "who was the greatest," Jesus called them together and said,

> "Whoever wants to be first must be last of all and servant of all."

> Then he took a little child and put it among them; and taking it in his arms, he said to them, "Whoever welcomes one such child in my name welcomes me, and whoever welcomes me welcomes not me but the one who sent me." (Mark 9:35b-37; cf., Matthew 18:1-5; Luke 9:46-48, NRSV)

This teaching didn't penetrate the hierarchical, adult-oriented brains of the disciples very well, and a little further down the road, Jesus had to stop another argument among the disciples about their authority in the kingdom of heaven:

> "You know that among the Gentiles those whom they recognize as their rulers lord it over them, and

their great ones are tyrants over them. But it is not so among you; but whoever wishes to become great among you must be your servant, and whoever wishes to be first among you must be slave of all. For the Son of Man came not to be served but to serve, and to give his life a ransom for many." (Mark 10:42b-45, NRSV; Matthew 20:20-28)

The world is familiar with domination and submission. It is even familiar with the rhetoric of service that hypocritically masks a will to power. But what does community life look like where greatness means submission to all?

Again, it is the Apostle Paul who understands the implications of Jesus' teaching best. In the Letter to the Ephesians where he teaches that the inclusiveness of the church reveals the great mystery of Christ, Paul gives the general rule of mutual submission under God:

Be kind to one another, tenderhearted, forgiving one another, as God in Christ has forgiven you. . . . Be subject to one another out of reverence for Christ. (Ephesians 4:32; 5:21, NRSV)

In the rest of the letter, he works out how this applies to the previously dominant relationships of men over women, parents over children, and masters over slaves.

Mutual submission is not incidental to salvation. It is the *only* way in which the community can avoid substituting human rule for the rule of the living word of God. Paul, like Jesus, expects mutual submission to be the hallmark of the community of faith. If there have been places and times where human beings have established hierarchical rule in the church of Christ with, for instance, monarchial episcopacies or authoritarian cults, they have been betrayals of Jesus' proclamation that the kingdom of God is at hand. Even democratic forms of congregational governance, when one faction dominates another, fall short of the unity possible under true mutual submission. Jesus came to ransom us all from such tyranny.

The second step in restoring the immediate rule of God is to make room in the course of community life for the living God to be heard. As the Apostle Paul traveled throughout the Mediterranean world, he organized the communities of Jesus' followers by this principle. In Chapters 12-14 of his First Letter to the Corinthians, Paul explained how God expresses his rule in the church through the distribution of the gifts of the Holy Spirit. At the center of his instruction is a discourse on love. Love is the antidote that leeches the poison from authority. "Love is patient; love is kind; love is not envious or boastful or arrogant" (1 Corinthians 13:4, NRSV).

With love at the center, Paul insists that the Holy Spirit has been poured out on all. The gifts of the Spirit are for everyone who believes; they are the gift of God and they are the key to the organization of the life of the community. As Paul tells the Corinthians:

> Now concerning spiritual gifts, brothers and sisters, I do not want you to be uninformed. . . .
>
> To each is given the manifestation of the Spirit for the common good. To one is given through the Spirit the utterance of wisdom, and to another the utterance of knowledge according to the same Spirit, to another faith by the same Spirit, to another gifts of healing by the one Spirit, to another the working of miracles, to another prophecy, to another the discernment of spirits, to another various kinds of tongues, to another the interpretation of tongues.

> All these are activated by one and the same Spirit,
> who allots to each one individually just as the Spirit
> chooses. (1 Corinthians 12:1, 7-11, NRSV)

Just as the distribution of judges among the tribes of Israel
was an expression of God's rule in an earlier time, so in the
time of the new covenant the Spirit distributes gifts according
to God's good pleasure. This is how God exercises sovereign
dominion over the church.

As with the gifts, so flows ministry within the body—never
as a hierarchy or appointed "office," but as the natural (or rather supernatural) consequence of the movement of the Holy
Spirit:

> first apostles, second prophets, third teachers; then
> deeds of power, then gifts of healing, forms of assis-
> tance, forms of leadership, various kinds of tongues.
> (1 Corinthians 12:28, NRSV)

Are these roles static—once expressed, always specific to certain individuals? Surely not in Paul's view, for he urges the
whole community to "strive for the greater gifts." (1 Corinthians 12:31, NRSV) Authority does not come with office in the
church; authority resides in the living word of God, expressed
through the Spirit—a Spirit free, as ever, to blow "where it
chooses" (John 3:8, NRSV) and characterized by love.

Finally, Paul insists that in the worship life of the community there must be space in which to receive the authoritative
presence of God in the exercise of these gifts. Here is a rare
glimpse into worship in the new covenant community:

> What should be done then, my friends? When you
> come together, each one has a hymn, a lesson, a rev-
> elation, a tongue, or an interpretation. Let all things

be done for building up. If anyone speaks in a tongue, let there be only two or at most three, and each in turn; and let one interpret. But if there is no one to interpret, let them be silent in church and speak to themselves and to God.[4]

Let two or three prophets speak, and let the others weigh what is said. If a revelation is made to someone else sitting nearby, let the first person be silent. For you can all prophesy one by one, so that all may learn and all be encouraged. (1 Corinthians 14:26-31, NRSV)

Paul is painting a picture of the community gathered for worship. It is a diverse community, and each one comes to worship with an offering of scripture or song or music or prayer. During the worship, the community expects that the Holy Spirit will move several different members (male or female, slave or free!) to speak prophetically in the name of the Risen Lord Jesus, as if he were present among them. And so he is, or else his promise, "I am with you always!" (Matthew 28:20, NRSV) is void.

Prophetic speech is not a matter of wild ecstasy, for "the spirits of prophets are subject to the prophets" (1 Corinthians 14:32, NRSV). Instead, it is a response to the compelling inward knowledge of the word of God implanted in the heart, such as impelled the prophets of the Old Testament (Jeremiah 1:9; 20:9; Amos 3:8; 7:15). It is simply and extraordinarily the gift of truthfully saying, "thus says the Lord." The rest of the community is silent and judges whether or not the word being spoken is authentically from God. Is the word we are hearing the truth of God? Does it reflect the grace we have seen in Jesus?[5]

Here, in the expectant silence of the community, Jesus is present as living Teacher and Lord (John 13:13), speaking anew to the community of faith, with just the same authority as when he taught his disciples in the flesh. Through the inspiration of the Holy Spirit, Christian prophets speak in the name of the risen Lord. Here the words of such an anonymous Christian prophet are recorded in the Book of Revelation:

> "Listen! I am standing at the door, knocking; if you hear my voice and open the door, I will come in to you and eat with you, and you with me." (Revelation 3:20, NRSV; see also 1 Corinthians 7:10 and 1 Thessalonians 4:15 for other examples of the prophetic mandate.)

To use the word, "I" when speaking for God, is the astonishing prerogative of the prophet.

The danger of such claim to prophetic authority is obvious. The third of the Ten Commandments is addressed to those who would falsely appropriate the name of God to authorize their own willful desires and schemes:

> You shall not make wrongful use of the name of the Lord your God, for the Lord will not acquit anyone who misuses his name. (Exodus 20:7, NRSV; Deuteronomy 5:11)

The history of Israel was rife with the problem of people who falsely claimed prophetic authority. (E.g., Deuteronomy 13:1-5; 18:20; 1 Kings 22:6ff; Isaiah 30:10; Jeremiah 5:31; 23:21)

The Christian community also confronted this problem, both when outsiders confronted the church (Acts 13:6) and, more troubling, from within. Perhaps it is inevitable that a community that exists by the living word of God will be af-

flicted by those who pretend to prophetic authority but do not
have it. Jesus himself warned strenuously, "many false prophets will arise and lead many astray" (Matthew 24:11, NRSV;
Mark 13:22; cf., Matthew 7:15). John and Peter both admon-
ished against undiscerning credulity:

> Beloved, do not believe every spirit, but test the spir-
> its to see whether they are from God; for many false
> prophets have gone out into the world. (1 John 4:1,
> NRSV)

> But false prophets also arose among the people, just
> as there will be false teachers among you, who will
> secretly bring in destructive opinions. (2 Peter 2:1,
> NRSV)

When Paul told the worshipers in Corinth to "weigh" the
words of the prophets, this is what he had in mind. Paul did
not ask the community "to ponder" or "learn from" its prophets
or teachers. Rather, in using the word "weigh," Paul is recalling
the rule of the judges over Israel. This is the same word that
Moses used of his work as a judge over the people (Exodus
18:16), and that Solomon used in his prayer for ability "to discern between good and evil" (I Kings 3:9, NAS). This is the
word Paul uses for the responsibility of the members of the
community to make judgments within the church when there
are disputes (1 Corinthians 6:5) and later for "discernment of
spirits" (1 Corinthians 12:10, NAB). It is, in short, the ability to recognize the authentic voice of God that Jesus spoke
of when he asserted that his followers "know . . . the voice" of
the Good Shepherd (John 10:4-5, NRSV). This authority to
discern rests in the hands of the entire community.

So, Paul provides for mutual submission even within the
worship life of the church. The community of faith weighs

what is said to confirm that the word that is spoken is not a
figment of the speaker's own imagination, a deception of the
fallen culture, or a self-interested attempt by the prophet to
manipulate the gullible, but is, indeed, the word of God. If it
is, the church offers confirmation, saying, "Amen."

The most detailed demonstration of the exercise of mutual submission recorded in scripture was the response of the
church to the controversy that surrounded Paul's teaching
about the inclusiveness of the chosen people. Paul was sure
that he had been inspired by the Holy Spirit and commissioned by God to preach this message. But it is a radical message, and in the early days of the Christian movement it was
not clear to everyone that Paul was right.

This was one of the first great tests of the unity of the new
covenant church.[6] Could people be saved (Acts 15:1) without
accepting the requirements of the law, particularly circumcision for the men? Paul's view flies in the face of a clear scriptural requirement, which states:

> Any uncircumcised male who is not circumcised
> in the flesh of his foreskin shall be cut off from his
> people; he has broken my covenant. (Genesis 17:14,
> NRSV).

If the matter had been decided on the basis of the authority of
this verse, the mystery of inclusion certainly would have been
denied, and Christianity would have become a soon-forgotten
sect within Judaism.

Acts 15 reports how the church struggled with the valid-
ity of Paul's claims of a new revelation from God. Paul and
his companion Barnabas were appointed by the believers in
Antioch (where the controversy first caused a crisis) to travel
to Jerusalem to consult with the "apostles and elders." In the

lengthy debate, all sides were heard. Barnabas and Paul described how they had seen evidence of the Holy Spirit coming to Gentile believers, to which some believers "who belonged to the sect of the Pharisees" responded that, nevertheless: "It is necessary for them to be circumcised and ordered to keep the law of Moses" (Acts 15:5, NRSV).

The Apostle Peter spoke out of his experience (recorded in Acts 10) of having been amazed to see the manifestation of the Holy Spirit among the Gentiles when he had preached at Cornelius' house—even though they did not follow the dietary laws. James recalled a passage about the last days from the prophet Amos which announced God's intention that "all other peoples may seek the Lord—even all the Gentiles" (Acts 15:17, NRSV; cf., Amos 9:11-12). From this James concluded that the church should not put obstacles in the way of the new believers.

After long consideration, Acts reports:

> Then the apostles and the elders, with the consent of the whole church, decided. . . . (Acts 15:22a, NRSV)

Finally, they wrote a letter to the church in Antioch in which they reported they had "decided unanimously" concerning the matter (Acts 15:25, NRSV), and that the decision "seemed good to the Holy Spirit and to us" (Acts 15:28, NRSV). The rule was mutual submission—even for James and Peter and Paul, even though they were the elders and apostles. The "whole church" came to unity under the ultimate authority, which, in the new covenant, is the living word of God.

The decision was that all were welcome, but that they should refrain from blood, food sacrificed to idols, and from sexual immorality/*porneia*. The necessity of ritual circumcision was abandoned. Both inclusiveness and righteousness were maintained—grace and truth held together in godly tension.

The Jerusalem assembly in Acts 15 demonstrates a way of discerning the truth, of walking by faith.

> 1) All views are heard. There can be no prior assumption that one group or another has all—or none—of the truth.

> 2) The freedom and authority of the Holy Spirit is honored in the living experience of the community of believers.

> 3) Scripture is consulted to assure continuity with God's work of salvation in history, but specific proof-texts are handled with care, interpreting them in light of major biblical themes.

> 4) The decision is made by elders and apostles—those whom the community recognize as having a special closeness to the person and ministry of Jesus.

> 5) The church must give its assent; the kingdom of God is expressed in the mutual submission of the whole people of God.

This may appear to be an extraordinarily fragile form of government. From a human point of view, it is. Servanthood and submission echo the weakness of the cross:

> For the message about the cross is foolishness to those who are perishing, but to us who are being saved it is the power of God. (1 Corinthians 1:18, NRSV)

### *The Throne of God and of the Lamb*

When God graciously declares that our sin is forgiven, the result is that our alienation from Paradise is ended and the *qol Yahweh* is heard again in our hearts. Loneliness is overcome, a people is formed who are first the recipients of God's love and, consequently, God's agents in the ministry of reconciliation (2 Corinthians 5:18). The community continues to grow—breaking down the barriers of hatred that sinful judgment concerning good and evil had built up.

The community is formed and held together by one thing only: the living word of God:

> In the beginning was the Word, and the Word was with God, and the Word was God.... And the Word became flesh and lived among us, and we have seen his glory, the glory as of a father's only son, full of grace and truth. (John 1:1, 14, NRSV)

It is this Word, who is the Light of the world (John 1:4; 8:12; 12:36). He says of himself, "And I, when I am lifted up from the earth, will draw all people to myself" (John 12:32, NRSV).

The vision of salvation is a revelation of New Jerusalem, gates open, and the nations streaming in:

> And the city has no need of sun or moon to shine on it, for the glory of God is its light, and its lamp is the Lamb. The nations will walk by its light, and the kings of the earth will bring their glory into it. Its gates will never be shut by day—and there will be no night there. (Revelation 21:23-25, NRSV)

The gates are open to the inclusive community. The only question for those who seek entrance is this: Are you willing to yield to God the right to judge good and evil? For around the throne of God are those who have agreed that they will give up this right. As they throw down the crowns of their petty kingdoms, they enter into the joyful community of God's beloved:

> At once I was in the spirit, and there in heaven stood a throne, with one seated on the throne! . . . Around the throne are twenty-four thrones, and seated on the thrones are twenty-four elders, dressed in white robes, with golden crowns on their heads. . . . Around the throne, and on each side of the throne, are four living creatures. . . . Day and night without ceasing they sing, "Holy, holy, holy, the Lord God the Almighty, who was and is and is to come."
>
> And whenever the living creatures give glory and honor and thanks to the one who is seated on the throne, who lives forever and ever, the twenty-four elders fall before the one who is seated on the throne and worship the one who lives forever and ever; they cast their crowns before the throne, singing, "You are worthy, our Lord and God, to receive glory and honor and power, for you created all things, and by your will they existed and were created." (Revelation 4:2, 4, 6, 8-11, NRSV)

The first sign of salvation is the restoration of the kingdom of God in the inclusive community that listens together to the living Word.

[1] The parable appears in different settings in Luke and Matthew. In Luke, Jesus tells the story in response to the Pharisees and the scribes who had grumbled, "'This fellow welcomes sinners and eats with them'" (Luke 15:2, NRSV). The point was that the community of salvation has to expand to include sinners. In Matthew, the parable introduces instructions about church discipline (Matthew 18:14ff), which then fleshes out the text: "it is not the will of your Father in heaven that one of these little ones should be lost." In either case, the essential point remains the same: the community needs to bend over backwards to rescue individuals from their alienation from God and, if possible, restore them to full membership in the community of the beloved.

[2] The good news is that what ultimately matters is attending to the voice of the Good Shepherd. Even those who, for whatever reason of history or culture, have not been able to receive the story of God's appearance in the history of Jesus and the cross, can respond to God's voice speaking in their hearts. This does not contradict Jesus' own words, "I am the way, and the truth, and the life. No one comes to the Father except through me" (John 14:6, NRSV) because Jesus is the Good Shepherd no matter whether the history of his life, death and resurrection is known or not known. When Jesus says those words in the Gospel of John, he says them as the Word who was with God from the beginning (John 1:1); Jesus is stating the fact that all who come to God do so through the agency of the word/*logos*. He is not saying "only those who make a specific confession of faith can come to God."

The universality of the promise of a new heart, and of the pouring out of the Holy Spirit, and of the assertion that the Light which is Christ "enlightens everyone" (John 1:9, NRSV), together with Jesus' own words, "whoever speaks a word against the Son of Man will be forgiven" (Matthew 12:32, NRSV; Luke 12:10; cf., Mark 2:28) overwhelm the legalistic supposition that salvation depends on a correct verbal confession. Likewise, it would be a mistake to conclude from Paul's affirmation in Romans 10:9, "if you confess with your lips that Jesus is Lord and believe in your heart that God raised him from the dead, you will be saved" (NRSV), that he believed that any specific verbal affirmation was sufficient for salvation. Paul is clear that the transformation of the heart that comes when the individual accepts God's inward revelation is of the essence. The institution of the church is composed of those who joyfully recognize Jesus as the agent of that transforming power. Sooner or later those who know the voice of the Good Shepherd *will* confess Jesus is Lord when they discover his true identity. The mysterious and invisible church of Christ is composed of all those who have inwardly heard and obeyed the word/*logos* whether or not they have known of or acknowledged the historical Jesus as their savior in this life. According to Jesus, we are in for some surprises when we meet our neighbors in the New Jerusalem!

[3] The passage later in the letter about women keeping silent in the church (1 Corinthians 14:34) must be read in tension with the general permission for women to minister given here. I am convinced that Paul was concerned to restore order to a situation where prophets were interrupting each another (14:27) and general discussions and disputations were breaking out during the course of worship (14:35). His prohibitions against disorderly speech during worship was directed as much to men as to women. See the following note.

[4] Note that in this passage, just as Paul expects that male and female should be free to speak according to the movement of the Spirit, so he also expects that—male or female—they will be silent when the Spirit is not moving them to speak in tongues or prophecy. The principle that people should speak in worship only as they are inspired by the Holy Spirit is what is at stake in the controversial passage about women being silent in the church, 1 Corinthians 4:34.

[5] There are three main scriptural criteria for judging prophets: (1) right confession, i.e., they testify to Jesus as Lord, and to God as God has been revealed in scripture (1 John 4:2; Deuteronomy 13:1ff; 1 Corinthians 12:3: Galatians 1:8f; 1 John 4:1ff; Revelation 19:10); (2) fulfillment of the word, when the prophecy is in the form of prediction (Deuteronomy 18:22; Isaiah 44:7f); and (3) right conduct (Isaiah 28:7f; Matthew 7:16f; 24:11), particularly that the true prophet never asks for money (Micah 3:5; 1 John 2:3-7).

A tract from early in the second century A.D., written from the perspective of something like a hundred years of experience of organizing community life on the basis of the living word of God, dealt at length with the question of traveling prophets and apostles. After saying that such a one should be welcomed "as if he were the Lord," the teaching continues:

> However, not everybody making ecstatic utterances is a prophet, but only if he behaves like the Lord. It is by their conduct that the false prophet and the [true] prophet can be distinguished. . . . Again, every prophet who teaches the truth but fails to practice what he preaches is a false prophet. But every attested and genuine prophet who acts with a view to symbolizing the mystery of the Church, and does not teach you to do all he does, must not be judged by you. His judgment rests with God. For the ancient prophets too acted in this way. But if someone says in the Spirit, "Give me money, or something else," you must not heed him. However, if he tells you to give for others in need, no one must condemn him.
>
> Everyone "who comes" to you "in the name of the Lord" must be welcomed. Afterward, when you have tested him, you will find out about him, for you have insight into right and wrong. If it is a traveler who arrives, help him all you can. But he must not stay with you more than two days, or, if necessary, three. If he wants to settle with you and is an artisan, he must work for his living. If, however, he has no trade, use your judgment in taking steps for him to live with you as a Christian without being idle. If he refuses to do this, he is trading on Christ. You must be on your guard against such people.

(*The Teaching of the Twelve Apostles, Commonly Called the Didache*, Chapters 11-12, in *Early Christian Fathers*, edited and translated by Cyril C. Richardson, Macmillan Publishing Co, New York: 1970, 176-177.)

[6] Acts 6:1-6 records an earlier test to the unity of the church when the believers who came from outside of Palestine believed that they were being short-changed in the distribution of goods by the Apostles who, of course, were all from Palestine. The re-

sponse of the church was a remarkable example of mutual submission and servanthood: the Apostles appointed a group of sev-
en deacons to take over the distribution, and, from their names, it
appears that all of them were from outside Palestine. They seem
to have decided, in effect, to yield complete authority to that faction of the community that was feeling oppressed.

# THE SIGN OF THE
# BOUNTIFUL COMMUNITY

*T*he listening community of the people of God is also, necessarily, a bountiful community because the One whose voice they listen to proclaims:

> "I am the bread of life. Whoever comes to me will never be hungry, and whoever believes in me will never be thirsty." (John 6:35, NRSV)

With these words, Jesus explained the meaning of the miracle of the multiplication of the loaves and fishes: he is, in himself, the source of prosperity and generosity. It is no wonder, then, that the great symbol of Jesus' presence is the banqueting table.

## The Mystery of Prosperity

> O Lord, how manifold are your works!
>   In wisdom you have made them all;
>   the earth is full of your creatures.
> . . . . . . . . . . . . . . . . . . . . . . . . . . . . . .
> These all look to you
>   to give them their food in due season;
> when you give to them,

> they gather it up;
> when you open your hand,
> they are filled with good things.
>
> > (Psalm 104:24, 27-28, NRSV)

Ultimately, God the Creator is the one who provides for the needs of all. If there is well-being, if there is *shalom*, it comes from God. Israel acknowledges this in its worship.

To express this, the law frequently commands the people to offer a "sacrifice of well-being" in thanksgiving to God (see Leviticus 7:13 and passim, NRSV). Some versions translate this sacrifice as, "peace offerings," because the underlying Hebrew word is *shalom*. The Greek version of the Old Testament invariably refers to these sacrifices as "offerings of salvation/*soterion*." God's saving work includes preserving us from scarcity and want.

The Psalmist reminds us that we do not offer sacrifices because of the neediness of God, but because we need to express thanks to God:

> "For every wild animal of the forest is mine,
> the cattle on a thousand hills.
> I know all the birds of the air,
> and all that moves in the field is mine.

> "If I were hungry, I would not tell you,
> for the world and all that is in it is mine.
> Do I eat the flesh of bulls,
> or drink the blood of goats?
> Offer to God a sacrifice of thanksgiving,
> and pay your vows to the Most High.
> Call on me in the day of trouble;
> I will deliver you, and you shall glorify me."

. . . . . . . . . . . . . . . . . . . . . . . . . . . . . . . . . . . . . .

"Those who bring thanksgiving as their sacrifice
honor me;
   to those who go the right way
   I will show the salvation of God."
(Psalm 50:10-15, 23, NRSV)

God desires only our free love. The material prosperity that
God brings to needy men and women evokes offerings of well-
being/*soterion* in an endless cycle of gratitude and overflowing
love.

Appropriately enough, the prophetic vision for the final era
of God's salvation, when death is "swallowed up," is also a vision of the banqueting table:

On this mountain the Lord of hosts will make for
   all peoples
  a feast of rich food, a feast of well-aged wines,
  of rich food filled with marrow, of well-aged wines
   strained clear.
And he will destroy on this mountain
  the shroud that is cast over all peoples,
  the sheet that is spread over all nations;
  he will swallow up death forever.
Then the Lord God will wipe away the tears from
   all faces,
  and the disgrace of his people he will take away
   from all the earth,
  for the Lord has spoken.
(Isaiah 25:6-8, NRSV)

The people around Jesus experienced the realization of this
vision when he raised the widow's son at Nain and when he
provided the rich wine at the wedding of Cana.

All along, God has intended the community of God's people to experience foretastes of the heavenly banquet. The com-

mandments of Sabbath and tithing are practice grounds for this. When the law is written on our hearts in the new covenant we find that we no longer experience Sabbath and tithe as gloomy obligations; instead we are freed to experience them as foretastes of paradise.

Among the Ten Commandments, the Sabbath commandment uniquely recalls the great act of salvation with which God liberated Israel from slavery in Egypt. It provides for rest and stands forever as a protest against an economy that would reduce human beings—or any of creation—to the status of commodities to be exploited in the interest of production. The command to rest is not only for the wealthy ones but for the servant and alien and the male and female slave and even for the donkey and other livestock because

> "you were a slave in the land of Egypt, and the Lord your God brought you out from there with a mighty hand." (Deuteronomy 5:15, NRSV)

The Sabbath is that time and place in which we recover our humanity and our fundamental status as creatures made in the image of God, not cogs in a machine.

Willingness to rest is also a great statement of faith in God as the source of prosperity. By resting, a person shows that she or he has been saved from the gnawing fear of scarcity, the inner compulsion to toil without ceasing.

If the Sabbath provides for rest, the tithe provides for fun. Far from being an onerous tax, the law of tithing originally called for an extravagance of feasting. God requires us to take a portion of our God-given wealth and use it to throw a great party. The law required the people to take the first fruits of the harvest to the Temple (or, if distance makes this inconvenient, to sell the produce) and

> go to the place that the Lord your God will choose;
> spend the money for whatever you wish—oxen,
> sheep, wine, strong drink, or whatever you desire.
> And you shall eat there in the presence of the Lord
> your God, you and your household rejoicing togeth-
> er. (Deuteronomy 14:25-26, NRSV)

What a commandment: spend your tithe money on whatever
you desire—so long as it is for the party! Here is no room
for prissy, disapproving religion—this is a celebration for the
great of heart in the presence of the God of abundant life.

The law of tithing was never selfish. The priests (who had
no part in the distribution of land among the twelve tribes of
Israel) and the poor are not neglected:

> Every third year you shall bring out the full tithe
> of your produce for that year, and store it within
> your towns; the Levites, because they have no allot-
> ment or inheritance with you, as well as the resident
> aliens, the orphans, and the widows in your towns,
> may come and eat their fill so that the Lord your
> God may bless you in all the work that you under-
> take. (Deuteronomy 14: 28-29, NRSV)

The picture is clear. With the tithe, as with the Sabbath, all
the people, rich and poor, are to enjoy rest and feasting together—a community bound together in a foretaste of the feast of
paradise.

The heavenly banquet—expressive of God's abundant
love and provision, particularly for the poor—was a constant
theme in Jesus' teaching about the kingdom of God. It was in-
credible that, in the busyness of daily life, people would choose
to ignore the simple joy that God had ordained.

Jesus told this story:

"Someone gave a great dinner and invited many. At the time for the dinner he sent his slave to say to those who had been invited, 'Come; for everything is ready now.'

"But they all alike began to make excuses. The first said to him, 'I have bought a piece of land, and I must go out and see it; please accept my regrets.' Another said, 'I have bought five yoke of oxen, and I am going to try them out; please accept my regrets.' Another said, 'I have just been married, and therefore I cannot come.'

"So the slave returned and reported this to his master. Then the owner of the house became angry and said to his slave, 'Go out at once into the streets and lanes of the town and bring in the poor, the crippled, the blind, and the lame.' And the slave said, 'Sir, what you ordered has been done, and there is still room.' Then the master said to the slave, 'Go out into the roads and lanes, and compel people to come in, so that my house may be filled. For I tell you, none of those who were invited will taste my dinner.'" (Luke 14:16-24, NRSV)

God is shouting: *please* stop being so busy all the time and, for goodness sake, *enjoy* yourselves!

Jesus' teaching was deeply rooted in the history of God's acts of salvation. The first great act of deliverance for the family of Abraham's descendents was rescue from famine. God used the mean-spirited jealousy of the sons of Jacob, who sold their brother Joseph into slavery, to place Joseph in a position to rescue both Egypt and the Hebrews from a devastating seven-year famine. Raised from slavery to become overseer of all of Pharaoh's business, Joseph was alerted to the coming famine by his divinely-inspired understanding of Pharaoh's dreams. He

> gathered up all the food of the seven years when
> there was plenty in the land of Egypt, and stored up
> food in the cities; he stored up in every city the food
> from the fields around it. So Joseph stored up grain
> in such abundance—like the sand of the sea—that
> he stopped measuring it; it was beyond measure.
> (Genesis 41:48-49, NRSV)

Here is godly abundance!

What happens next is archetypical of God's work in salvation. In an astonishing act of generosity and reconciliation, Joseph rescues his brothers (not to mention the alien, slaveholding nation of Egypt). The grain—abundant beyond measure—becomes a sign of salvation when coupled with reconciliation and generosity. The capstone is Joseph's comment to his brothers:

> You intended to harm me, but God intended it for
> good to accomplish what is now being done, the saving of many lives. (Genesis 50:20, NIV)

God's grace proved greater than human sin.

With the coming of a new dynasty and the passage of time, the Hebrew people were enslaved. The book of Exodus records God's second great act of deliverance on their behalf, a deliverance that came in two parts. The first part was the physical deliverance from enemies at the Passover and at the Red Sea. The second part was their psychological deliverance from a slave mentality.

This had many facets, but one of the most important focused on issues of materialism.

> The whole congregation of the Israelites complained
> against Moses and Aaron in the wilderness. The

> Israelites said to them, "If only we had died by the
> hand of the Lord in the land of Egypt, when we sat
> by the fleshpots and ate our fill of bread; for you have
> brought us out into this wilderness to kill this whole
> assembly with hunger." (Exodus 16:2-3, NRSV)

Instead of reacting negatively to the yearning of the people for
the comforts of their enslavement, God saw that their need
was real and acted in a miraculous way to show them that their
salvation extended to their material needs as well:

> The Lord spoke to Moses and said, "I have heard the
> complaining of the Israelites; say to them, 'At twi-
> light you shall eat meat, and in the morning you shall
> have your fill of bread; then you shall know that I am
> the Lord your God.'" In the evening quails came up
> and covered the camp; and in the morning there was
> a layer of dew around the camp. When the layer of
> dew lifted, there on the surface of the wilderness was
> a fine flaky substance, as fine as frost on the ground.
> When the Israelites saw it, they said to one another,
> "What is it?" For they did not know what it was.
> Moses said to them, "It is the bread that the Lord
> has given you to eat. . . . " The house of Israel called
> it *manna*; it was like coriander seed, white, and the
> taste of it was like wafers made with honey. (Exodus
> 16:11-15, 31, NRSV)

Time and again, as they wandered the desert before entering the land of promise, God miraculously saved them. When
Jesus broke bread with his followers and miraculously fed the
crowds, multiplying the loaves and fishes so that all would be
satisfied, he continued this strain of God's gracious provision.

## The Countersign of Jubilee

Wealth, in itself, is an ambivalent sign. Wealth can point to the blessings of God, or it can point to the exploitation of the poor by an oppressor class. It is important to remember that God provides for all; but it is equally important to remember that God has a special concern for the poor. The history of salvation, from the Exodus through the prophets, shows this. The laws of Sabbath and tithing expressly call for the poor to be included in the community of God's prosperity. When the poor are excluded, God rises up to save them:

> "Because the poor are despoiled,
>   because the needy groan,
> I will now rise up," says the Lord;
>   "I will place them in the safety for which
>     they long."
>
> (Psalm 12:5, NRSV)

The "place of safety" translates the words for salvation (Hebrew *yesha*; Greek *soteria*). The place of safety is the community where the prosperity of God is known, not just by an elite, but by all. The English word "economy" derives from the Greek word *oikonomia*, the management of a household. The place of safety into which God intends to move the needy ones is the household of God's people, where poverty and oppression are no more.

In the extraordinary law of the Sabbath year, God requires the community to end economic oppression—to save the poor—by means of the cancellation of debts:

> Every seventh year you shall grant a remission of debts. And this is the manner of the remission: every creditor shall remit the claim that is held against a neighbor, not exacting it of a neighbor who is a

member of the community, because the Lord's remission has been proclaimed. . . .

If there is among you anyone in need, a member of
your community in any of your towns within the
land that the Lord your God is giving you, do not
be hard-hearted or tight-fisted toward your needy
neighbor. You should rather open your hand, willingly lending enough to meet the need, whatever it
may be. Be careful that you do not entertain a mean
thought, thinking, "The seventh year, the year of
remission, is near," and therefore view your needy
neighbor with hostility and give nothing; your
neighbor might cry to the Lord against you, and you
would incur guilt.

Give liberally and be ungrudging when you do so,
for on this account the Lord your God will bless you
in all your work and in all that you undertake. Since
there will never cease to be some in need on the
earth, I therefore command you, "Open your hand
to the poor and needy neighbor in your land." (Deuteronomy 15:1-2, 7-11, NRSV)

Leviticus 25 has a variation on this law of release and generosity:

in the seventh year there shall be a Sabbath of complete rest for the land, a Sabbath for the Lord: you
shall not sow your field or prune your vineyard. (Leviticus 25:4, NRSV)

What a triumph! The curse of scarcity is reversed; even the
land is allowed to rest and, thereby, to be restored. God assures
the people that in the sixth year the land will provide plenty
to carry the people through the Sabbath year and still provide

seed for the following year. By lying fallow, the restored earth can respond with the added generosity that God intends. The law of Sabbath is a glory of rest, of feasting, of economic restoration for body and soul, for the human community, for the environment—in short, for the entire *oikonomia*.

On top of this, God adds a special "jubilee." The jubilee is the fiftieth year, a year of economic revolution. On the occasion of the seventh sabbatical year, the commandment reads:

> Then you shall have the trumpet sounded loud; on the tenth day of the seventh month—on the day of atonement—you shall have the trumpet sounded throughout all your land. And you shall hallow the fiftieth year and you shall proclaim liberty throughout the land to all its inhabitants. It shall be a jubilee for you: you shall return, every one of you, to your property and every one of you to your family. (Leviticus 25:9-10, NRSV)

In this way, God explicitly adds an economic dimension to the day of atonement which had been set aside for cleansing the land of sin (Cf., Leviticus 16).

When the law instructs, "you shall return . . . to your property," it is not just for a visit. This is a great "land reform": all the land of Israel is to be redistributed, so that each family has restored to it land that it originally received as the tribes entered the Promised Land (see Joshua 13-19). Over the years, for whatever reason, the family may have sold or lost their inheritance. Never mind! God's intention is that each family should return to their "inheritance" because the land is the basis for their economic freedom.

At the root of all this is the principle that the land does not actually belong to its human "owners," but to God:

> When you make a sale to your neighbor or buy
> from your neighbor, you shall not cheat one another.
> When you buy from your neighbor, you shall pay
> only for the number of years since the jubilee; the
> seller shall charge you only for the remaining crop
> years. . . . The land shall not be sold in perpetuity, *for
> the land is mine*; with me you are but aliens and ten-
> ants. (Leviticus 25:14-15, 23, NRSV, my emphasis)

God's intent for that time as well as for today is clear: the
jubilee prohibits the accumulation of economic power in the
hands of a few at the expense of the many. There is the freedom of property ownership and a market economy, but that
freedom is circumscribed by the basic principle that an independent economic base for each extended family must be assured. When debts are cancelled in the seventh year, and land
redistributed in the fiftieth year, the poor have a chance to
start again. The law is especially clear that debt-slavery is to
be remitted.[1] As the commandment acknowledges, there will
always be poverty in this world, but God's will is that "there
should be no poor among you" (Deuteronomy 15:4, NIV). At
least there will not be poor in the sense of an oppressed class,
perpetually doomed to servitude by the economic system.

Unfortunately, throughout the history of Israel, at least as
recorded in the scriptures, there is no evidence that the law
of jubilee was implemented. Instead, with increasing urgency,
the prophets cry out on behalf of God's concern for the poor.
Isaiah attributes the calamities of the Assyrian invasion of 733
B.C. to this:

> The Lord enters into judgment with the elders and
> princes of his people: It is you who have devoured
> the vineyard; the spoil of the poor is in your hous-

es. What do you mean by crushing my people, by grinding the face of the poor? says the Lord God of hosts.

Ah, you who join house to house, who add field to field, until there is room for no one but you, and you are left to live alone in the midst of the land!

Therefore my people go into exile without knowledge; their nobles are dying of hunger, and their multitude is parched with thirst. Therefore Sheol [i.e., the place of death] has enlarged its appetite and opened its mouth beyond measure; the nobility of Jerusalem and her multitude go down, her throng and all who exult in her. (Isaiah 3:14-15; 5:8, 13-14, NRSV)

But the leaders did not learn. At the initiation of the prophet Jeremiah—a generation after the calamity of the exile of the Northern kingdom—there was an abortive attempt at reform according to the jubilee law. But it was soon betrayed by the selfishness of the rich. Jeremiah records the tragic history:

The word of the Lord came to Jeremiah from the Lord: Thus says the Lord, the God of Israel: I myself made a covenant with your ancestors when I brought them out of the land of Egypt, out of the house of slavery, saying, "Every seventh year each of you must set free any Hebrews who have been sold to you and have served you six years; you must set them free from your service." But your ancestors did not listen to me or incline their ears to me. You yourselves recently repented and did what was right in my sight by proclaiming liberty to one another, and you made a covenant before me in the house that is called by my name; but then you turned around and profaned my name when each of you took back your male and female slaves, whom you had set free according to their desire, and you brought them again into subjection to be your slaves.

Therefore, thus says the Lord: You have not obeyed me by granting a release to your neighbors and friends; I am going to grant a release to you, says the Lord—a release to the sword, to pestilence, and to famine. I will make you a horror to all the kingdoms of the earth. (Jeremiah 34:12-17, NRSV)

In God's eyes, and now in the sight of the nations, the sign of prosperity had become a sign of horror because of the failure of the people of God to be faithful to the poor. For this failure, God goes on to proclaim the great exile: "I will hand them over . . . to the army of the king of Babylon" (Jeremiah 34:21, NRSV). In the crucial aspect of economic justice, God says, the people have "transgressed my covenant" (Jeremiah 34:18, NRSV).

Even so, both Jeremiah and Ezekiel—prophesying during the exile to the captives in Babylon—hold out the promise that prosperity will, one day, be restored and that this, too, will be a sign to the nations:

And this city shall be to me a name of joy, a praise and a glory before all the nations of the earth who shall hear of all the good that I do for them; they shall fear and tremble because of all the good and all the prosperity I provide for it. (Jeremiah 33:9, NRSV)

Their hope for renewed prosperity has now become entwined with the hope of a new covenant, the gift of a new heart (see Ezekiel 36:26-36), and the promise of the Good Shepherd who will overcome the oppression of the poor:

> Therefore, thus says the Lord God to them: I myself
> will judge between the fat sheep and the lean sheep.
> Because you pushed with flank and shoulder, and
> butted at all the weak animals with your horns until
> you scattered them far and wide, I will save my flock,
> and they shall no longer be ravaged; and I will judge
> between sheep and sheep. I will set up over them one
> shepherd, my servant David, and he shall feed them:
> he shall feed them and be their shepherd. (Ezekiel
> 34:20-23, NRSV)

Ezekiel's allegory informs Jesus' claim to be that Good
Shepherd:

> "The thief comes only to steal and kill and destroy. I
> came that they may have life, and have it abundantly.
> I am the good shepherd." (John 10:10-11, NRSV)

The community of which Jesus is the Good Shepherd is
necessarily a community of economic justice. When economic
justice is not present, that is a sign that false shepherds have
once again broken in to scatter the flock.

When John the Baptist wanted to know if Jesus was, in fact,
the promised Messiah, he sent his disciples to inquire. Jesus
replied:

> "Go and tell John what you have seen and heard: the
> blind receive their sight, the lame walk, the lepers
> are cleansed, the deaf hear, the dead are raised, the
> *poor have good news brought to them.*" (Luke 7:22b,
> NRSV, my emphasis)

The good news that Jesus preached to the poor was that
the kingdom of God was at hand, in his person and in the
life of the community of his disciples. A central sign of this is
the renewed practice of Sabbath and jubilee: the forgiveness

of debts. The evidence of this is scattered throughout Jesus' teaching, but nowhere more emphatically than in the prayer that he taught his disciples:

> Father, hallowed be your name,
>   your kingdom come.
> Give us each day our daily bread
>   and forgive us our sins
> for we ourselves forgive everyone in debt to us,
>   and do not subject us to the final test.
>     (Luke 11:2b-4, NAB; Matthew 6:9-13)[2]

In Jesus' prayer, the plea to God for forgiveness of sin is predicated on the assumption that those who are praying are themselves already practitioners of the forgiveness of debts. In speaking of debtors, Jesus uses the very word that appeared in Deuteronomy 15:2 for the Sabbath year remission of debts.

In his prayer, Jesus brackets the petition about forgiveness by references to God's economic provision. The pleas for "daily bread" and for preservation from God's "test" come straight from the story of God's provision of *manna* in the wilderness in Exodus 16:

> Then the Lord said to Moses, "I am going to rain bread from heaven for you, and *each day* the people shall go out and gather enough for that day. In that way I will *test* them, whether they will follow my instruction or not. (Exodus 16:4, NRSV, my emphasis)

The promise, very literally, was for daily bread. What was the test? The test was that the people were to gather enough for each day's need and no more. The one exception—because they were not to gather on the Sabbath—was that on the day before the Sabbath they were to gather enough for two days.

> The Israelites did so, some gathering more, some less. But when they measured it with an omer, those who gathered much had nothing over, and those who gathered little had no shortage; they gathered as much as each of them needed. And Moses said to them, "Let no one leave any of it over until morning." But they did not listen to Moses; some left part of it until morning, and it bred worms and became foul. (Exodus 16:17-20a, NRSV)

Daily bread—the bread from heaven—is the mystery of God's provision. There is always enough! But in our anxiety lest that "enough" might not really be enough, we scrabble and toil to build up a reserve against the day when we fear the "enough" of God will fail. That hoarding of the world's goods is the root of economic oppression.

What is at issue here is practical faith. Do people have faith in the loving provision of God, the Creator and owner of all that is? Or, by their actions, will people demonstrate that they believe that God cannot, or will not, provide? Reliance on daily bread is a test—and, in this prayer, Jesus suggests that it is an ultimate test—of human faith in the love and power of God to save. Because it demonstrates lack of faith in the goodness of God and God's ability to provide "daily bread," hoarding of goods and building up of reserves amount to practical atheism, if not worship of another god.

This is why Jesus casts the issue in terms of a choice of allegiance between two masters: God and *mammon*.

> "Do not store up for yourselves treasures on earth, where moth and rust consume and where thieves break in and steal; but store up for yourselves treasures in heaven, where neither moth nor rust consumes and where thieves do not break in and steal. For where your treasure is, there your heart will be also. . . .

"No one can serve two masters; for a slave will either hate the one and love the other, or be devoted to the one and despise the other. You cannot serve God and wealth/*mammon*." (Matthew 6:19-21, 24, NRSV)34

Perhaps that is also why the Apostle Paul called greed "idolatry" (Colossians 3:5-6, NRSV; cf., 1 Timothy 6:9-10), and why the prophet Elijah battled so fiercely against the worship of the Canaanite fertility God Baal (1 Kings 18).

If hoarding is idolatry, and the practice of the Sabbath year and Jubilee provisions is its opposite, how does the voluntary community of God's kingdom live out God's economic salvation? With this parable, Jesus begins to answer this question:

And he said to them, "Take care! Be on your guard against all kinds of greed; for one's life does not consist in the abundance of possessions."

Then he told them a parable: "The land of a rich man produced abundantly. And he thought to himself, 'What should I do, for I have no place to store my crops?' Then he said, 'I will do this: I will pull down my barns and build larger ones, and there I will store all my grain and my goods. And I will say to my soul, "Soul, you have ample goods laid up for many years; relax, eat, drink, be merry." But God said to him, 'You fool! This very night your life is being demanded of you. And the things you have prepared, whose will they be?' So it is with those who store up treasures for themselves but are not rich toward God." (Luke 12:15-21, NRSV)

The important thing is to understand what Jesus means when he speaks of being "rich toward God."

Jesus inaugurated his movement in a country occupied by a Roman empire officially committed to the idolatrous worship of Caesar and with the connivance of a local ruling class that had—willingly or not—undertaken a policy of cooperation. Part of that cooperation involved a massive system of taxation to support the cost of the military occupation (a system particularly well known through the story of Joseph and Mary going to Bethlehem to "be enrolled" at the time of Jesus' birth). This system of taxation included ample opportunities for graft, but it certainly did not include a schedule of release from debts.

Part of Jesus' response to this situation was to recruit these very "traitors" into the fellowship of salvation. The Apostle Matthew was, of course, precisely one of those enemies of the people whom Jesus turned into a friend:

> As Jesus was walking along, he saw a man called Matthew sitting at the tax booth; and he said to him, "Follow me." And he got up and followed him.
>
> And as he sat at dinner in the house, *many tax collectors* and sinners came and were sitting with him and his disciples. When the Pharisees saw this, they said to his disciples, "Why does your teacher eat with tax collectors and sinners?" But when he heard this, he said, "Those who are well have no need of a physician, but those who are sick. Go and learn what this means, 'I desire mercy, not sacrifice.' For I have come to call not the righteous but sinners." (Matthew 9:9-13, NRSV, my emphasis)

The call of Matthew—the tax collector—was not a chance encounter; it was Jesus' habit to dine with collaborators, part of a deliberate strategy for extending the jubilee aspect of the kingdom of God. It would be delightful to have a transcript of the conversations that took place around those banqueting tables, to see how Jesus wooed the servants of *mammon* away from their false faith to faith in God.

Fortunately, in the story of Zacchaeus, we have the details of just such an assault on *mammon's* stronghold in the region of Jericho:

> He entered Jericho and was going through the town and suddenly a man whose name was Zacchaeus made his appearance; he was one of the senior tax collectors and a wealthy man. He kept trying to see which Jesus was, but he was too short and could not see him for the crowd; so he ran ahead and climbed a sycamore tree to catch a glimpse of Jesus who was to pass that way. When Jesus reached the spot he looked up and spoke to him, 'Zacchaeus, come down. Hurry, because I am to stay at your house today.' And he hurried down and welcomed him joyfully.
>
> They all complained when they saw what was happening. 'He has gone to stay at a sinner's house,' they said. But Zacchaeus stood his ground and said to the Lord, 'Look, sir, I am going to give half my property to the poor, and if I have cheated anybody I will pay him back four times the amount.' And Jesus said to him, 'Today salvation has come to this house, because this man too is a son of Abraham; for the Son of man has come to seek out and save what was lost.' (Luke 19:1-10, NJB)

Who was looking for whom? Of course, Zacchaeus climbed the tree looking for Jesus—and this may indicate that Zacchaeus had been hearing about Jesus through his own network of fellow collaborators—but it was Jesus who said, "I *am to* stay in your house," as if this were his predetermined plan. Despite the grumbling of the crowd against Jesus for dining with Zacchaeus, Zacchaeus "stood his ground," which turned out to be the ground of economic justice and the remission of debts. Zaccheaus has responded to the coming of the kingdom of God in the presence of Jesus by implementing the Jubilee. Jesus' exclamation, "Salvation has come to this house," a cry of triumph over another stronghold of *mammon*.

Jesus' strategy extends to people much farther down the pecking order of society than Zacchaeus or even Matthew. He lays out the plan in a humorous parable that Luke uses to introduce Jesus' teaching about the impossibility of serving both God and *mammon*:

> Now He was also saying to the disciples, "There was a certain rich man who had a steward, and this steward was reported to him as squandering his possessions. And he called him and said to him, 'What is this I hear about you? Give an account of your stewardship, for you can no longer be steward.'

> "And the steward said to himself, 'What shall I do, since my master is taking the stewardship away from me? I am not strong enough to dig; I am ashamed to beg. I know what I shall do, so that when I am removed from the stewardship, they will receive me into their homes.'

> "And he summoned each one of his master's debtors, and he began saying to the first, 'How much do you owe my master?' And he said, 'A hundred measures of oil.' And he said to him, 'Take your bill, and sit down quickly and write fifty.' Then he said to another, 'And how much do you owe?' And he said, 'A hundred measures of wheat.' He said to him, 'Take your bill, and write eighty.'

> "And his master praised the unrighteous steward because he had acted shrewdly; for the sons of this age

> are more shrewd in relation to their own kind than
> the sons of light. And I say to you, make friends for
> yourselves by means of the *mammon* of unrighteous-
> ness; that when it fails, they may receive you into the
> eternal dwellings. (Luke 16:1-9, NAS)

Beyond the comedy, there is a general principle that Jesus
wants to convey. His disciples are to take "the *mammon* of
unrighteousness" and convert it into the instrument of God's
blessing. How people may do that is as varied as the circumstances of life. In the end, this is what Jesus means by "being
rich toward God."

It would be foolish indeed to suppose that Jesus does not
mean it when he uses the language of salvation, of idolatry,
and of eternal life in speaking of our relationship with wealth.
It is recorded that one day a man ran up to Jesus and, kneeling
before him, asked, "What must I do to inherit eternal life?"
(Mark 10:17b, NRSV). Jesus recited from the list of the Ten
Commandments, and the man responded that he had observed all these from his childhood. Then,

> Jesus, looking at him, loved him and said, "You lack
> one thing; go, sell what you own, and give the money
> to the poor, and you will have treasure in heaven;
> then come, follow me." (Mark 10:21, NRSV; Mat-
> thew 19:21; Luke 18:22)

The one thing lacking was the tenth item in the list of commandments that Jesus had not yet named: "You shall not covet
. . ." (Exodus 20:17, NRSV; Deuteronomy 5:21). This is the
only one of the ethical commandments to speak of a condition
of the heart. The young man in fact had not "stolen," nevertheless, his heart had been stolen by *mammon*.

Jesus looked at him with love, hoping for him the same joy

he encountered in Zacchaeus. Jesus was offering, at that moment, the gift of a new heart. But this unnamed man "went away grieving," because his possessions owned him and he could not find it within himself to declare the jubilee release. So he turned down Jesus' invitation to "Come, follow me" and join in the new covenant community.[4]

Why did the young man go away "grieving"? He may or may not have been grieving for his soul, but surely he was sad to miss out on the joyful company that surrounded Jesus. When he ran up to Jesus to ask him about eternal life, this is what he saw:

> [Jesus] went on through cities and villages, proclaiming and bringing the good news of the kingdom of God. The twelve were with him, as well as some women who had been cured of evil spirits and infirmities: Mary, called Magdalene, from whom seven demons had gone out, and Joanna, the wife of Herod's steward Chuza, and Susanna, and many others, who provided for them out of their resources. (Luke 8:1-3, NRSV)

This wild company of itinerant men and women had accepted Jesus' invitation of freedom from bondage to *mammon*, and were living out the experience of God's bountiful community. Judas held the common purse (John 13:29). When their monetary resources did not seem sufficient to meet the needs of the moment, Jesus was in their midst to multiply the little they had (Luke 9:10ff; Matthew 14:13ff; Mark 6:31ff; 8:11ff; John 6:1ff; cf., Acts 3:6), because he is "the true bread from heaven" (John 6:32, NRSV). It was the invitation to join in this joyful community that the young man turned down.

After Jesus' resurrection and the pouring out of the Holy Spirit on the church in Jerusalem at Pentecost, the disciples

prayed that God would grant them boldness and would perform "signs and wonders . . . through the name of your holy
servant Jesus" (Acts 4:30, NRSV). One of the signs and wonders that followed was the continuation of Jesus' joyful community of the common purse:

> Now the whole group of those who believed were
> of one heart and soul, and no one claimed private
> ownership of any possessions, but everything they
> owned was held in common. With great power the
> apostles gave their testimony to the resurrection
> of the Lord Jesus, and great grace was upon them
> all. There was not a needy person among them, for
> as many as owned lands or houses sold them and
> brought the proceeds of what was sold. They laid it
> at the apostles' feet, and it was distributed to each as
> any had need. (Acts 4:32-35, NRSV)

The observation that "there was not a needy person among
them," of course, is a direct claim that in the apostolic church
the Sabbath year law of remission of debts where "there should
be no poor among you," found in Deuteronomy 15:4, is fulfilled.

The story of Ananias and Sapphira that follows underlines
the significance of this to the church (Acts 5:1-11). They were
wealthy Christians who understood the imperative of the jubilee as a sign of salvation. They sold their property but, instead
of handing all the proceeds over to the apostles for the common distribution, they kept back some for their own private
use. In short, they were hedging their bet about the providence
of God. Their deceit was immediately discovered and God miraculously punished them—by taking their lives. The seriousness of the penalty reveals the seriousness of the offense. It was

not just that they lied; in this particular lie they were breaking covenant with God in a manner parallel to the rulers in Judah in the time of Jeremiah who had promised to implement the jubilee release of debt-slaves but did not do so.

The particular method by which the community of faith lives out the jubilee will vary in time and circumstance. But it must be lived out. The common purse, in itself, is not necessarily a sign of salvation, but the presence of the bountiful community is. In the concluding parable in the Gospel of Matthew, Jesus says that the decisive issue at the final judgment will be how we have treated the poor—"the least of these who are members of my family." On this hinges "eternal punishment" or "eternal life" (Matthew 25:31-46, NRSV). Jesus could not have made the stakes any higher.

As Paul went about his commission of establishing the church of Christ throughout the Mediterranean world, we find him busy carrying out this imperative, organizing a collection for the poor during a time of famine in Jerusalem (Romans 15:26; 2 Corinthians 8:1-9:15; Acts 11:27-30). In writing to the church at Corinth about this collection, Paul lays out perfectly the law of God's abundance, quoting from the Exodus account of the provision of *manna*:

> I do not mean that there should be relief for others and pressure on you, but it is a question of a fair balance between your present abundance and their need, so that their abundance may be for your need, in order that there may be a fair balance. As it is written, "The one who had much did not have too much, and the one who had little did not have too little." (2 Corinthians 8:13-15, NRSV; cf., Exodus 16:8)

## The Marriage Feast of the Lamb

In the end, we have returned to God's heavenly banquet, laid out for us on God's holy Mountain, a sure feature of God's new covenant.

> Ho, everyone who thirsts, come to the waters; and you that have no money, come, buy and eat! Come, buy wine and milk without money and without price. Why do you spend your money for that which is not bread, and your labor for that which does not satisfy? Listen carefully to me, and eat what is good, and delight yourselves in rich food. Incline your ear, and come to me; listen, so that you may live. I will make with you an everlasting covenant, my steadfast, sure love for David. (Isaiah 55:1-3, NRSV)

The cost is only this: a faith in God that implies rejection of the sway of *mammon* over our lives. At the end of the Book of Revelation, before we cross the sea of fire into the New Jerusalem and come to the tree of life whose leaves are for the healing of the nations, there is the feast of the Lamb, the symbol of the joyous fellowship of the church and the spirit of abundance in which we are to live.

Just prior to that, John relates this vision of the destruction of Babylon—which he called "Mystery Babylon" (Revelation 17:5, NIV) because it is the symbol of a culture ruled by *mammon*—where materialism and greed have ground the faces of the poor:

> After this I saw another angel coming down from heaven, having great authority; and the earth was made bright with his splendor. He called out with a mighty voice, "Fallen, fallen is Babylon the great! It has become a dwelling place of demons, a haunt of

every foul spirit, a haunt of every foul bird, a haunt of every foul and hateful beast. For all the nations have drunk of the wine of the wrath of her fornication, and the kings of the earth have committed fornication with her, and the merchants of the earth have grown rich from the power of her luxury. . . . "

And the merchants of the earth weep and mourn for her, since no one buys their cargo anymore, cargo of gold, silver, jewels and pearls, fine linen, purple, silk and scarlet, all kinds of scented wood, all articles of ivory, all articles of costly wood, bronze, iron, and marble, cinnamon, spice, incense, myrrh, frankincense, wine, olive oil, choice flour and wheat, cattle and sheep, horses and chariots, slaves—and human lives. . . .

The merchants of these wares, who gained wealth from her, will stand far off, in fear of her torment, weeping and mourning aloud, "Alas, alas, the great city, clothed in fine linen, in purple and scarlet, adorned with gold, with jewels, and with pearls! For in one hour all this wealth has been laid waste!"

And all shipmasters and seafarers, sailors and all whose trade is on the sea, stood far off and cried out as they saw the smoke of her burning, "What city was like the great city?" And they threw dust on their heads, as they wept and mourned, crying out, "Alas, alas, the great city, where all who had ships at sea grew rich by her wealth! For in one hour she has been laid waste. . . . " For your merchants were the magnates of the earth, and all nations were deceived by your sorcery. And in you was found the blood of prophets and of saints, and of all who have been slaughtered on earth." (Revelation 18: 1-3, 11-13, 15-19, 23b-24, NRSV)

John the Revelator saw the connection between luxurious living, global systems of concentrated wealth, and the violence of imperialistic war. He knew it for what it was: the curse of Satan over the world that merits God's wrath and will receive God's judgment. Personal salvation is inseparable from God's judgment on oppressive economic systems, because our personal salvation brings us into the life God intended from the beginning of creation.

Sweat shops, child labor, women and children economically forced into prostitution or suffering sexual abuse and exploitation in their homes, slavery of all kinds, societies where social stratification means that the wealthiest five per cent of the population controls the vast majority of the God-given wealth of the community, all of which breeds war and violent crime — these are signs of the curse.

Let the church of Jesus Christ not call good what God has called evil. Let the church of Jesus Christ heed the cry of the Angel in John's vision:

> Then I heard another voice from heaven saying, "Come out of her, my people, so that you do not take part in her sins, and so that you do not share in her plagues; for her sins are heaped high as heaven, and God has remembered her iniquities. (Revelation 18:4-5, NRSV)

The life of the church is to boycott the luxurious economics of oppression while celebrating the Jubilee economics of God's abundance that is symbolized by Jesus' banqueting table.

The destruction of the great merchants and their kings is immediately followed by this great hymn of salvation:

> After this I heard what seemed to be the loud voice of a great multitude in heaven, saying, "Hallelujah!

Salvation and glory and power to our God, for his judgments are true and just; . . .

Then I heard what seemed to be the voice of a great multitude, like the sound of many waters and like the sound of mighty thunderpeals, crying out, "Hallelujah! For the Lord our God the Almighty reigns. Let us rejoice and exult and give him the glory, for the marriage of the Lamb has come, and his bride has made herself ready; to her it has been granted to be clothed with fine linen, bright and pure"—for the fine linen is the righteous deeds of the saints.

And the angel said to me, "Write this: Blessed are those who are invited to the marriage supper of the Lamb." And he said to me, "These are true words of God." (Revelation 19:1-9, NRSV)

The marriage supper of the Lamb is the abundance, creative work and joyful celebration of love that God intended for humanity from the beginning of creation, lived in simplicity of heart and marked by lavish generosity and sharing. The bounty of the community of God's people is a sign of salvation.

---

[1] The details of how this works out is offered in Leviticus 25:25-55, which prohibits debt slavery in Israel—at least for Israelites; freedom for debt-slaves is made a Sabbath year requirement in Deuteronomy 15:12-17.

[2] The biblical version of the prayer uses specifically economic terminology. The New American Bible translation used here clearly reveals the relationship between "daily bread," "debt," and "test." However, the adjective "final" before "test" is not supported by the Greek and is interpretive. This test may indeed be of ul-

timate significance, but Jesus did not have the final judgment in mind.

The elaborated form of the prayer familiar from church services derives from the *Didache* (*op. cit.*) The version of the prayer often used in liturgies, which replaces "debts" and "debtors" with "trespasses" and "those who trespass against us," has virtually no textual support, but appears in the third century writings of Origen (apparatus of the Nestle-Aland *Novum Testamentum Graece*, 26 edition).

³ In the middle of this passage comes the somewhat obscure teaching:

> "The eye is the lamp of the body. So if your eye is healthy [*aplous*, single], your whole body will be full of light; but if your eye is unhealthy [*poneros*, evil], your whole body will be full of darkness. If then, the light in you is darkness, how great is the darkness!"(Matthew 6:22-23, NRSV).

There are some intriguing connections with other texts that concern economics: first through the eye which is evil or unhealthy, and then in the prophetic concern for single-hearted devotion to God.

In Matthew 20:1-15, Jesus offers a parable about the landowner who hires laborers to work in his "vineyard" (always a symbol of the kingdom of God). He offers to pay them a denarius (the day's wage, i.e., daily bread). Some work all day, others arrive late and work only part of the day, but the landowner pays them all their denarii as promised. The workers who were hired first complain, and the landowner responds, "are you envious because I am generous?" (Matthew 20:15b, NRSV). NRSV footnotes provide a more literal translation, "is your eye evil/*poneros* because I am good?" The unhealthy eye (the eye that is not single, but that is divided between God and *mammon*) is envious and unsatisfied with the provision of daily bread—no matter how adequate it may be!

As we have seen above, Jeremiah associated the failure to follow through with the Sabbath and Jubilee laws with the breaking of the covenant (Jeremiah 34:18; cf., Ezekiel 22:6-15). Later, during the catastrophe of the Babylonian captivity both Jeremiah and Ezekiel addressed the exiles and promised a renewal of the covenant. Both associated that renewal with renewed prosperity.

The "single eye" of Jesus' discourse is reminiscent of Jeremiah's promise that the renewed covenant will come with the gift of a "single heart."

> "I will give them one heart and one way, that they may fear me for all time, for their own good and the good of their children after them. I will make an everlasting covenant with them.... For thus says the LORD: Just as I have brought all this great disaster upon this people, so I will bring upon them all the good fortune that I now promise them." (Jeremiah 32:39-42, NRSV)

The single eye and the single heart are gifts of God. They speak to the same promise that came through Ezekiel of the gift of "a new heart ... and a new spirit." (Ezekiel 36:26, NRSV) Ezekiel also promised that the new heart would be accompanied with restored prosperity that would, in turn, be a sign to the nations of God's saving power:

> And they will say, "this land that was desolate has become like the garden of Eden; and the waste and desolate and ruined towns are now inhabited and fortified." Then the nations that are left all around you shall know that I, the LORD, have rebuilt the ruined places, and replanted that which was desolate; I the LORD, have spoken, and I will do it. (Ezekiel 36:35-36, NRSV)

Jesus was not directly alluding to these passages from Jeremiah and Ezekiel when he spoke about a "single eye" and an "evil eye." However, the relationship developed by the prophets between single-hearted devotion to God and issues of wealth serves as important interpretive background to explain how the "eye" passage fits into Jesus' discourse on God vs. *mammon*. Singleness of devotion to God is a condition for receiving the blessings of God's providence and means open-heartedness to others and concern for their well-being.

[4]In the conversation between Jesus and his disciples that follows this encounter there is an interesting, if faint, allusion to the story of covenant breaking and renewal in Jeremiah. When Jesus goes on to say how hard it will be for the rich to enter the

kingdom, the disciples ask, "Then who can be saved?" Jesus responds, "For mortals it is impossible, but not for God; for God all things are possible" (Mark 10:26-27, NRSV; Luke 18:26-27; Matthew 19:25-26). This echoes God's promise, in Jeremiah, of the restoration of prosperity to Jerusalem after the exile: "See, I am the LORD, the God of all flesh; is anything too hard for me?" (Jeremiah 32:27, NRSV).

# THE SIGN OF THE
# PEACEABLE COMMUNITY

*I*n the Book of Revelation, the same "Mystery Babylon" that is bloated with luxury is described as being "drunk with the blood of the saints and the blood of the witnesses to Jesus" (Revelation 17:5-6, NIV). Mystery Babylon is known, above all, for those two things: the exploitation of the poor by the rich and the use of political power to imprison and kill God's people.

When the church of Christ has gone astray, reformers have risen up to decry "the Babylonian captivity of the church." There are two primary signs of this captivity and they correspond to these two features of Mystery Babylon. The first sign that the church has fallen captive is that the people of God seek security and well-being in riches instead of God's miraculous provision of daily bread. The second sign of the captivity of the church is that the people of God employ political and military violence, instead of relying upon the miraculous power of God to deliver them from their enemies.

Just as faith in God as the One who provides daily bread frees the community of God's people to practice a life of joyful simplicity and generosity, so faith in God as warrior on behalf of the oppressed frees the community of God's people to live a life of love and forgiveness as befits the children of God. In both cases, the underlying issue is idolatry, and salvation is at stake.

The biblical record is full of the wars of God's people. From the original assault on the promised land to the wars of the kings of Israel and Judah, we find the people in bloody battle—often instigated and sanctioned by God. Behind all of this, however, lies a truth that only comes into its fullness in the new covenant: the warfare of God's people is to be fought by God alone. This truth is embedded in the holy war tradition,[1] and it is here that we find the language of salvation.

In these verses, the psalmist puts the matter negatively:

> A king is not saved by his great army;
>   a warrior is not delivered by his great strength.
> The war horse is a vain hope for victory,
>   and by its great might it cannot save.
>       (Psalm 33:16-17, NRSV; cf., Psalm 44:4-7)

The prophet Zephaniah puts the same matter positively. At issue is the source of justice, relief from oppression, healing for those who are hurt, and victory for the nation. The prophet knows that these are all aspects of God's salvation:

> The Lord, your God, is in your midst,
>   a warrior who gives victory/*yasha*
> he will rejoice over you with gladness,
>   he will renew you in his love;
> he will exult over you with loud singing
>   as on a day of festival.
>
> I will remove disaster from you,
>   so that you will not bear reproach for it.
> I will deal with all your oppressors at that time.
> And I will save/*yasha* the lame

and gather the outcast,
and I will change their shame into praise
and renown in all the earth.
(Zephaniah 3:17-19, NRSV)

The hope of the people of God for justice and safety is not based on ignorance, or denial, of the reality of oppression and evil in the world. It is based on faith in God's power to save. The prophet Zechariah put it most succinctly: "Not by might, nor by power, but by my spirit, says the Lord of hosts" (Zechariah 4:6, NRSV).

### The Mystery of God as Warrior

God demonstrated this power to save by his Spirit alone, first and decisively, in the great act of deliverance of the enslaved Hebrews from Egypt. The exodus was marked by two great acts of warfare that were undertaken by God without human intervention. The first was the slaughter of all of Egypt's firstborn males (Exodus 12:29). It was this that finally provoked Pharaoh to let the Hebrew people go, an event celebrated annually in the Passover feast. But, before the escaping slaves had gotten far, Pharaoh repented of his decision and sent his army after them. Trapped between the sea and the greatest military force in the world, "in great fear, the Israelites cried out to the Lord" (Exodus 14:10b, NRSV).

In response to this cry, Moses gives the great secret of holy war:

> But Moses said to the people, "Do not be afraid, stand firm, and see the deliverance that the Lord will accomplish for you today; for the Egyptians whom you see today you shall never see again. The Lord will fight for you, and you have only to keep still." (Exodus 14:13-14, NRSV)

The secret is this: do not be afraid, stand firm, and God will do the fighting for you.

And so God did. The technique by which God wiped out Pharaoh and his army is not particularly important for it is likely never to be repeated. What is important is that, with the power that belongs alone to the creator of all that is, God delivered the escaping slaves from their oppressors:

> Thus the Lord saved Israel that day from the Egyptians; and Israel saw the Egyptians dead on the seashore. (Exodus 14:30, NRSV)

This sight evoked from Moses and Miriam the song of salvation which contains the great affirmation of faith, "Yahweh is a warrior; Yahweh is his name":

> "I will sing to the Lord, for he has triumphed
>    gloriously;
>   horse and rider he has thrown into the sea.
> The Lord is my strength and my might,
>   and he has become my salvation;
> this is my God, and I will praise him,
>   my father's God, and I will exalt him.
> The Lord is a warrior;
>   the Lord is his name.
> (Exodus 15:1b-3, NRSV)

Yahweh, it turns out, is jealous of his prerogative to fight on behalf of the oppressed. Even when, in those days before the new covenant, God used human instruments in battle against oppression, he insisted on making it clear to whom the victory belonged. In the time of King Jabin of Canaan, when his commander Sisera was oppressing the Israelites "cruelly" with "nine hundred chariots of iron," God appointed Deborah, a prophetess, to judge Israel, and arranged it so that the woman

Jael, rather than any of the male warriors of Israel, would kill Sisera (Judges 4).

God's choice of a woman to deliver Israel, of course, affirms the equality of men and women in God's eyes. More than that, in reversing the usual presumption of male strength and female weakness, it serves as a sign that the weakness of God is stronger than any human strength.

The next judge raised up by God was Gideon, whose story epitomizes God's attitude. The Midianites had been oppressing the Israelites, so Gideon raised an army to fight them off. God responds:

> "The troops with you are too many for me to give the Midianites into their hand. Israel would only take the credit away from me, saying, 'My own hand has delivered me.'" (Judges 7:2b, NRSV)

In standard holy war fashion, God instructs Gideon to send away the fearful, and anyone else who doesn't want to be there (cf., Deuteronomy 20:2-8).[2] Twenty-two thousand left, but ten thousand remained. That was still way too many. (Military strategists, of course, wouldn't think so; Israel was facing a force of 135,000, according to Judges 8:10). Following God's instructions, Gideon had the troops go to a stream to drink:

> "All those who lap the water with their tongues, as a dog laps, you shall put to one side; all those who kneel down to drink, putting their hands to their mouths, you shall put to the other side."

> The number of those that lapped was three hundred; but all the rest of the troops knelt down to drink water. Then the Lord said to Gideon, "With the three

> hundred that lapped I will deliver you, and give the
> Midianites into your hand. Let all the others go to
> their homes." (Judges 7:5b-7, NRSV)

Could there be a sillier notion of warfare than selecting
only the few really stupid troops who put down their weapons, got down on all fours, and lapped water from the river
like dogs,[3] while sending away the ones who stayed alert and
at the ready? But that was God's choice. Gideon then armed
them—not with swords, but with pots, torches, and trumpets!
Only then was God's army ready for a battle in which the victory would be credited to Yahweh alone.

Despite repeated evidence of God's power to save by raising
up charismatic judges, the people demanded a king and the
visible security of a standing army (1 Samuel 8:5b, NRSV).
In response Samuel—the last of the judges—offered these
prophetic words:

> "These will be the ways of the king who will reign
> over you: he will take your sons and appoint them
> to his chariots and to be his horsemen, and to run
> before his chariots; and he will appoint for himself
> commanders of thousands and commanders of fif-
> ties, and some to plow his ground and to reap his
> harvest, and to make his implements of war and the
> equipment of his chariots. He will take your daugh-
> ters to be perfumers and cooks and bakers. He will
> take the best of your fields and vineyards and olive
> orchards and give them to his courtiers. He will take
> one-tenth of your grain and of your vineyards and
> give it to his officers and his courtiers. He will take
> your male and female slaves, and the best of your
> cattle and donkeys, and put them to his work. He
> will take one-tenth of your flocks, and you shall be
> his slaves. And in that day you will cry out because

of your king, whom you have chosen for yourselves; but the Lord will not answer you in that day." (1 Samuel 8:11-17, NRSV)

The choice of the people to have a human king with all that entails (a standing army, military taxation and conscription, government bureaucracies to carry out the census that makes all this possible, social stratification with an elite class increasingly ensnared in luxuriousness) was a tragic rejection of the kingdom of God. Nevertheless, for many years, while the kings reigned, God continued to act as a warrior in defense of the people against their enemies.

The first instance was David's battle with the Philistine giant Goliath. By any analysis of the balance of power, Israel could not win. Yet, when David offered to stand against Goliath, he rejected armor and weaponry. The point was not that David was foolhardy. Neither was the point that he was courageous, strong, or really good with a sling shot. The point was the one he made to the heavily armed King Saul:

> "The Lord, who saved me from the paw of the lion and from the paw of the bear, will save me from the hand of this Philistine." (1 Samuel 17:37, NRSV)

His response to Goliath's taunts was even clearer:

> "You come to me with sword and spear and javelin; but I come to you in the name of the Lord of hosts ... so that all the earth may know that there is a God in Israel, that all this assembly may know that the Lord does not save by sword and spear; for the battle is the Lord's. ..." (1 Samuel 17:45-47, NRSV)

His humility and his faith in God's power to save were the chief sources of David's greatness.[4]

Some years later, when "a great multitude" of the Moabites and Ammonites (and some of the Meunites) attacked the southern kingdom of Judah during the reign of King Jehoshaphat, the king was afraid. He fasted and prayed:

> "O our God, will you not execute judgment upon them? For we are powerless against this great multitude that is coming against us. We do not know what to do, but our eyes are on you." (2 Chronicles 20:12, NRSV)

That was good praying! The answer came through the Levite, Jahaziel, son of Zechariah, in terms familiar from the Exodus:

> Thus says the Lord to you: 'Do not fear or be dismayed at this great multitude; for the battle is not yours but God's. Tomorrow go down against them; they will come up by the ascent of Ziz; you will find them at the end of the valley, before the wilderness of Jeruel.

> 'This battle is not for you to fight; take your position, stand still, and see the victory of the Lord on your behalf, O Judah and Jerusalem.' Do not fear or be dismayed; tomorrow go out against them, and the Lord will be with you." (2 Chronicles 20:15b-17, NRSV)

The people went out the next day, singing and praising God. This is what they saw: in great confusion, "the Ammonites and Moab . . . all helped to destroy one another" (2 Chronicles 10:23, NRSV).

The best of all the Yahweh battle stories took place a lit-tle later, in the time of Elisha, when the king of Aram was at war against the northern kingdom of Israel. Elisha's prophetic powers had provided Israel with military intelligence that pro-tected it from Aram's attacks. Aram was "greatly perturbed" by this, and he set out to attack the city where Elisha lived.

> When an attendant of [Elisha] the man of God, rose early in the morning and went out, an army with horses and chariots was all around the city. His ser-vant said, "Alas, master! What shall we do?"
>
> He replied, "Do not be afraid, for there are more with us than there are with them."
>
> Then Elisha prayed: "O Lord, please open his eyes that he may see." So the Lord opened the eyes of the servant, and he saw; the mountain was full of horses and chariots of fire all around Elisha. (2 Kings 6:15-17, NRSV; see also Joshua 5:13-15)

Most of the time the faithful, like Elisha's attendant, are blind to the power and majesty of God, but their eyes are open to see the strength of worldly opposition to the cause of God. Elisha's prayer reversed the usual course of things, and the eyes of the faithful were opened while the eyes of the enemy were blinded. If the vision of the reality of the hosts of Yahweh could take root in the minds of all God's people, how free they would be from fear—perhaps free enough even to renounce their reliance on human rulers with their puny armies.

> When the Arameans came down against him, Eli-sha prayed to the Lord, and said, "Strike this peo-ple, please, with blindness." So he struck them with blindness as Elisha had asked.

Elisha said to them, "This is not the way, and this is not the city; follow me, and I will bring you to the man whom you seek." And he led them to Samaria. As soon as they entered Samaria, Elisha said, "O Lord, open the eyes of these men so that they may see." The Lord opened their eyes, and they saw that they were inside Samaria.

When the king of Israel saw them he said to Elisha, "Father, shall I kill them? Shall I kill them?"

It is Elisha's answer to this question that delights, for it foreshadows Jesus' own ministry of reconciliation:

He answered, "No! Did you capture with your sword and your bow those whom you want to kill? Set food and water before them so that they may eat and drink; and let them go to their master." So he prepared for them a great feast; after they ate and drank, he sent them on their way, and they went to their master. And the Arameans no longer came raiding into the land of Israel. (2 Kings 6:18-23, NRSV)

In all these episodes, we hear the holy war instruction: do not be afraid, stand firm, and see the salvation God will bring. God, however, makes clear that the necessity of the people doing their part, namely trusting in God alone. This brings us to the countersign of Immanuel.

### *The Countersign of Immanuel*

One of the most famous and dramatic of the holy war stories comes from the time of the prophets Isaiah and Hosea. It recounts how God destroyed the army of Sennacherib of Assyria by plague when he was laying siege to Jerusalem (2 Chronicles 32:1-22). Years later, when Jeremiah instructed Judah to submit to Nebuchadnezzar's conquest, other prophets looked back to this history and God's promise to protect Jerusalem (e.g., Isaiah 31:5-9; Hosea 1:7). They falsely announced, "peace, peace" for their generation (Jeremiah 6:14; 8:11), and scoffed at Jeremiah's warning that this time God would allow Jerusalem to be destroyed. Where did this misunderstanding arise?

The false prophets seem to have forgotten another prophecy of Isaiah: the ominous word that he spoke foretelling the destruction of Judah. That prophecy was the first in which God proffered the sign of Immanuel.

It was 734 B.C. and Judah was under attack from Israel and Aram (Syria). In order to understand this story, it is helpful to recall the geopolitical situation. Solomon's kingdom had been split into two small kingdoms: Israel in the north (including the Sea of Galilee), and Judah in the south (including Jerusalem). These two little kingdoms were surrounded by hostile nations: Philistia (to the southwest); Edom, Moab, and Ammon (to the east); and Aram and Phoenicia (to the north). Aram (with its capital in Damascus) was the dominant kingdom, but lurking in the background was Assyria, the great empire stretching east to the Persian Gulf.

So, when King Ahaz of Judah heard that King Pekah of Israel had made a military alliance with King Rezin of Aram, he had good cause to worry. The threat was great, and while Jerusalem was under attack from this conspiracy in the north, a second front was opened in the southeast:

> Then King Rezin of Aram and King Pekah son of Remaliah of Israel came up to wage war on Jerusalem; they besieged Ahaz but could not conquer him. At that time the king of Edom . . . drove the Judeans from Elath. . . . (2 Kings 16:5-7, NRSV)

Elath was a city on the northern tip of the Red Sea that marked the southern extent of Judah. When Edom conquered Elath, that meant that Judah was reduced to almost half of its size. Worried by this loss of territory, and now under attack from both the north and the east, the king of Judah, King Ahaz, decided to seek help from Assyria, the super-power to the east.

> Ahaz sent messengers to King Tiglath-pileser of Assyria, saying, "I am your servant and your son. Come up, and rescue me from the hand of the king of Aram and from the hand of the king of Israel, who are attacking me." Ahaz also took the silver and gold found in the house of the Lord and in the treasures of the king's house, and sent a present to the king of Assyria. The king of Assyria listened to him; the king of Assyria marched up against Damascus, and took it, carrying its people captive to Kir; then he killed Rezin. (2 Kings 16:7-9, NRSV)

From the point of view of political realism, this is a history of great statesmanship. King Ahaz made a military alliance that pushed back a coordinated invasion from three enemy countries and secured peace for Jerusalem—at least for a time. Nevertheless, it is recorded in scripture as an utter defeat.

At the time of the initial conspiracy of Aram and Israel in the north against Judah, the prophet Isaiah had come to King Ahaz in Jerusalem. He gave the king a prophetic sign and assured him that God intended to protect Jerusalem. The sign was that a child was to be born who would be named Immanuel. (Isaiah 7:14) Immanuel, of course, means "God with us," and Isaiah was promising God's presence as warrior to save Judah from her enemies.

In terms again reminiscent of the Exodus event, Isaiah had delivered this word to Ahaz:

> "Take heed, be quiet, do not fear, and do not let
> your heart be faint because of these two smoldering
> stumps of firebrands. . . ." (Isaiah 7:4a, NRSV)

However, facing war from two nations to the north and one to
the east, Ahaz could not find it within himself to rely entirely
on God for protection. His lack of trust manifested itself in
idolatry. The scriptures record:

> [Ahaz] did not do what was right in the sight of
> the Lord his God, as his ancestor David had done,
> but he walked in the way of the kings of Israel. He
> even made his son pass through fire, according to
> the abominable practices of the nations whom the
> Lord drove out before the people of Israel. He sac-
> rificed and made offerings on the high places, on the
> hills, and under every green tree. (2 Kings 16:2b-4,
> NRSV)

In making offerings on the high places and making his son
pass through fire, Ahaz was worshipping the god Baal—also
known as Moleck,[5] and expressing his lack of faith in Yahweh
to save. Isaiah sees that, behind these symbolic acts of idolatrous worship, the practical expression of Ahaz's idolatry was
the military alliance he contracted with Assyria to defend Jerusalem against the conspiracy of Rezin and Pekah. It was in
forging that alliance that Ahaz effectively turned away from
allegiance to Yahweh.

Isaiah cried out:

> Do not call conspiracy all that this people calls con-
> spiracy, and do not fear what it fears, or be in dread.
> But the Lord of hosts, him you shall regard as holy;
> let him be your fear, and let him be your dread. He
> will become a sanctuary, a stone one strikes against;

> for both houses of Israel he will become a rock one
> stumbles over—a trap and a snare for the inhabit-
> ants of Jerusalem. And many among them shall
> stumble; they shall fall and be broken; they shall be
> snared and taken. (Isaiah 8:12-15, NRSV)

Mesmerized by fear and lured by the military strength of
Assyria, Ahaz rejected Yahweh and turned to an unfaithful
military alliance for salvation. In the eyes of the prophet, by
that act, Judah rejected God as its warrior as it had already
rejected him as king. Shortly afterward, Isaiah prophesied
again:

> Because this people has refused the waters of Shilo-
> ah that flow gently, and melt in fear before Rezin and
> the son of Remaliah; therefore, the Lord is bringing
> up against it the mighty flood waters of the River, the
> king of Assyria and all his glory; it will rise above all
> its channels and overflow all its banks; it will sweep
> on into Judah as a flood, and, pouring over, it will
> reach up to the neck; and its outspread wings will
> fill the breadth of your land, O Immanuel. (Isaiah
> 8:5-8, NRSV)

This is the prophecy of the destruction of Jerusalem and
Judah. In contrast with the earlier promise, now the cry, "O
Immanuel," God with us, has become a prophecy of the terrible Day of the Lord. The very empire to which Judah looked
for security turned out to be its destruction. This prophecy
was fulfilled in Jeremiah's time. Both houses of Israel stumbled
at the sign of Immanuel and, contracting a series of failed military alliances, were destroyed.[6]

Immanuel is the sign of God's presence as warrior to defend
us against our enemies. Immanuel is also the sign of judgment

against us should we choose to rely on human warfare instead of God.

Christians recognize in Jesus the fulfillment of the sign of Immanuel (Matthew 1:21-23).[7] Appropriately for one who is a sign of God's presence as a warrior, his birth was greeted by

> the multitude of the heavenly host, praising God
> and saying:
> 'Glory to God in the highest heaven,
>   and on earth peace among those whom he favors!'
>                               (Luke 2:13-14, NRSV)

Angels are terrible in their beauty and power: they are the spiritual army of God, the host that Elisha saw and showed his attendant when Israel was under attack. It is not for nothing that the shepherds were afraid when they saw these heralds of Jesus' birth.

As at the beginning of Jesus' life, so at its end we hear of angels of the heavenly host and words of peace on earth. At his arrest, when Peter started to fight on his behalf,

> Jesus said to him, "Put your sword back into its place; for all who take the sword will perish by the sword. Do you think that I cannot appeal to my Father, and he will at once send me more than twelve legions of angels?" (Matthew 26:52-53; cf., John 18:11, NRSV)

The coming of Immanuel is a countersign to humanity's rejection of the peace that the Lord of hosts/*sabaot* makes possible. Therefore, at the beginning of Jesus' ministry, John the Baptist emerges as the voice of one crying the word of peace in the wilderness:

> Comfort, comfort my people, says your God. Speak
> tenderly to Jerusalem, and cry to her that her war-
> fare/*sabaot* is ended, that her iniquity is pardoned,
> that she has received from the Lord's hand double
> for all her sins. A voice cries: "In the wilderness pre-
> pare the way of the Lord, make straight in the desert
> a highway for our God." (Isaiah 40:1-3, RSV; quot-
> ed in Matthew 3:3; Mark 1:2-3; Luke 3:4-6; John
> 1:23)

Our warfare is ended because Immanuel is here among us:
he is the sign of the presence of Yahweh *sabaot*—the Lord of
hosts who wars on our behalf.

Jesus' command to Peter to put up his sword was not a rejection of holy war; it was, instead, its fulfillment in the new
covenant. Jesus knew the choice had to be made either to rely
upon Yahweh and his hosts, or to follow the way of Molech
and sacrifice children to war. Jesus had made his decision, at
the very start of his ministry, when he rejected Satan's offer to
give him the splendor and power of the nations, "if you will fall
down and worship me." Jesus' answer was unequivocal:

> "Away with you, Satan! for it is written, 'Worship
> the Lord your God, and serve only him.'" (Matthew
> 4:8-10, NRSV; Luke 4:6-8; see also John 6:15.)[8]

Similarly, Jesus puts to his disciples the choice of following
God or Molech—just as he had confronted them with the
choice of God or *mammon*.

When he was on his way to Jerusalem some Samaritan vil-
lagers refused to offer Jesus hospitality.

> When his disciples James and John saw it, they said,
> "Lord, do you want us to command fire to come

down from heaven and consume them?" But he turned and rebuked them. (Luke 9:54-55, NRSV)

Some manuscripts continue with Jesus' words, "Ye know not what manner of spirit ye are of." (Luke 9:55, KJV) When they wanted to "bomb" the village for Jesus' sake, the disciples had rejected Yahweh and taken on the spirituality of Molech.

When Peter tried to dissuade Jesus from going on to Jerusalem where Jesus had announced he would suffer and ultimately be killed, Jesus' response was quick and harsh:

> "Get behind me, Satan! For you are setting your mind not on divine things but on human things." (Mark 8:33b, NRSV; Matthew 16:23)

Those who choose to be part of the new covenant kingdom of God must join Immanuel in relying on the saving power of Yahweh *sabaot*.[9]  In the kingdom of God inaugurated by Jesus, as at the time of the Exodus, warfare is entirely in God's hands. Jesus instructed his disciples in terms similar to those of Moses when he instructed the fleeing Hebrew slaves: do not be afraid, stand firm, the Lord will fight for you.

When Jesus instructed his disciples in their mission, he foretold the dangers they would face: he was sending them out like "sheep in the midst of wolves." But he reassured them with the promise that they would have the Spirit of God to rely upon:

> "they will hand you over to councils and flog you in their synagogues; and you will be dragged before governors and kings because of me, as a testimony to them and the Gentiles. When they hand you over, do not worry about how you are to speak or what

you are to say; for what you are to say will be given to
you at that time; for it is not you who speak, but the
Spirit of your Father speaking through you.

Do not fear those who kill the body but cannot kill
the soul; rather fear him who can destroy both soul
and body in hell. Are not two sparrows sold for a
penny? Yet not one of them will fall to the ground
apart from your Father. And even the hairs of your
head are all counted. So do not be afraid; you are of
more value than many sparrows. (Matthew 10:16-
20, 28-31, NRSV)

The context for Jesus' appearance as Immanuel was, of
course, the same context in which Jesus reasserted the Jubilee.
Faced by an overwhelming military occupation force, the Jewish people had one of three options: they collaborated (like
Matthew and Zaccheus); they took up arms (like Theudas and
Judas the Galilean in Acts 5:36-37); or they mutely suffered.
Jesus, however, offered a fourth way suitable to a kingdom that
was no longer defined by ethnic or political boundaries. He
taught them how to pray and how to perform prophetic signs,
and, finally, how to take up the cross. These were among the
practical tools Jesus gave his disciples to help them "stand firm"
while they awaited God's appearance as warrior on their behalf.

In the face of their mute suffering, Jesus gives his disciples
voice by teaching them to call upon Yahweh:

"Pray then in this way:
Our Father in heaven,
  hallowed be your name.
Your kingdom come.
  Your will be done,
  on earth as it is in heaven."
                  (Matthew 6:9-10, NRSV)

172

We have already seen how this prayer functioned in the context of the jubilee economics of the kingdom of God. Here, we see how it functions in the context of Immanuel's warfare. This prayer that God's reign be manifest on earth is essentially the same prayer as that of the Hebrew slaves confronted with Pharaoh's army and of King Jehoshaphat when he was faced with the multitude of Moabites and Ammonites. It cries out with the psalmist:

> Give justice to the weak and the orphan;
>   maintain the right of the lowly and the destitute.
> Rescue the weak and the needy;
>   deliver them from the hand of the wicked."
> . . . . . . . . . . . . . . . . . . . . . . . . . . . . . . . . . . . .
> Rise up, O God, judge the earth;
>   for all the nations belong to you!"
> (Psalm 82:3-4, 8, NRSV)

Knowing, as he does, that more than twelve legions of angels stand ready for the battle, Jesus is fearless as he goes about proclaiming that the kingdom of God is at hand. He seeks to transmit this fearlessness to his disciples, and so he taught them practical techniques for quenching fear and standing firm in the face of repression.

The Roman army had many prerogatives in the occupied territories. Jesus had these in mind when he taught:

> But I say to you, Do not resist an evildoer. But if anyone strikes you on the right cheek, turn the other also; and if anyone wants to sue you and take your coat, give your cloak as well; and if anyone forces you to go one mile, go also the second mile. (Matthew 5:39-41, NRSV)

Here were ways to stand firm in the face of the enemy. By will-fully exceeding their demands, the oppressed rob the oppressors of their power to terrify.[10] By demonstrating the humanity of the oppressed, they reach out to the conscience within the oppressor, and transform the relationship from dehumanized oppressed and dehumanized oppressor to that of person with person.

But these were more than clever techniques for reclaiming the initiative and transforming conflict. They were also prophetic signs of the salvation of God when human rights are denied. During the exile, Jeremiah had written:

> It is good that one should wait quietly for the salvation of the Lord. It is good . . . to give one's cheek to the smiter, and be filled with insults. For the Lord will not reject forever. . . . When all the prisoners of the land are crushed under foot, when human rights are perverted in the presence of the Most High, when one's case is subverted—does the Lord not see it? . . .
>
> Let us lift up our hearts as well as our hands to God in heaven. . . .
>
> Pay them back for their deeds, O Lord, according to the work of their hands! Give them anguish of heart; your curse be on them! Pursue them in anger and destroy them from under the Lord's heavens. (Lamentations 3:26-27, 30-31, 34-35, 41, 64-66, NRSV)

Read in the light of this tradition, the instruction, "turn the other cheek," contains within it a prophetic cry for God's vengeance against those who would violate the human rights of the poor. Jesus was certainly not telling the weak to cooperate in their oppression; he was giving them a sign of the spiritual warfare of God.

The boldest of Jesus' prophetic signs was his dramatic entry into Jerusalem and overturning of the tables of the money changers in the Temple (Matthew 21:1-17; Mark 11:1-18; Luke 19:29-46; John 2:12-23). This is the annual focus of Christian worship on Palm Sunday—the celebration of Jesus' appeal to God to renew his warfare on behalf of the oppressed.

When Jesus rode into Jerusalem on the back of the colt, he was acting out the apocalyptic vision found in Zechariah:

> Lo, your king comes to you;
>   triumphant and victorious is he,
> humble and riding on a donkey,
>   on a colt, the foal of a donkey.
> He will cut off the chariot from Ephraim
>   and the war horse from Jerusalem;
>                   (Zechariah 9:9b-10, NRSV)

Take note, oppressors! This is a song of the victory of the Lord of hosts. Zechariah continues the prophecy with this promise to the oppressed:

> As for you also, because of the blood of my
>       covenant with you,
>   I will set your prisoners free from the waterless
>       pit.
> . . . . . . . . . . . . . . . . . . . . . . . . . . . . . . . . . . . . .
> For I have bent Judah as my bow;
>   I have made Ephraim its arrow.
> I will arouse your sons, O Zion,
>   against your sons, O Greece,
>   and wield you like a warrior's sword.

> Then the Lord will appear over them,
>   and his arrow go forth like lightning;
> the Lord God will sound the trumpet
>   and march forth in the whirlwinds of the south.
> The Lord of hosts will protect them,
> . . . . . . . . . . . . . . . . . . . . . . . . . . . . . . .
> On that day the Lord their God will save them
>   for they are the flock of his people
> for like the jewels of a crown
>   they shall shine on his land.
>               (Zechariah 9:11, 13-16, NRSV)

Jesus' reenactment of Zechariah's vision was accompanied by the triumph song of Psalm 118. The Gospels quote this portion of it:

> Save us, we beseech you, O Lord!
> O Lord, we beseech you, give us success!
> Blessed is the one who comes in the name
>   of the Lord.
>         (Psalm 118:25-26a, NRSV; cf. Matthew 21:9;
>                   Mark 11:9; Luke 19:38)

Read in context, the Psalm is a mighty hymn to Yahweh's surprising victory when the people of God were surrounded by their foes:

> All nations surrounded me;
>   in the name of the Lord I cut them off!
> They surrounded me, surrounded me on every side;
>   in the name of the Lord I cut them off!
> They surrounded me like bees;
>   they blazed like a fire of thorns;
>   in the name of the Lord I cut them off!
> I was pushed hard, so that I was falling,
>   but the Lord helped me.
> The Lord is my strength and my might;
>   he has become my salvation.

There are glad songs of victory in the tents
  of the righteous:
"The right hand of the Lord does valiantly;
the right hand of the Lord is exalted;
the right hand of the Lord does valiantly."
                    (Psalm 118:10-16, NRSV)

With this hymn of Yahweh, Lord of hosts, ringing in his
ears, Jesus proceeded into the Temple to overturn the tables of
the money changers. This too was a symbolic act, recalling the
words of a prophet, for as he "cleansed the Temple," Jesus cried
out words from Jeremiah:

> Has this house, which is called by my name, be-
> come a den of robbers in your sight? You know, I
> too am watching, says the Lord. (Jeremiah 7:11,
> NRSV; quoted in Matthew 21:13, Mark 11:17,
> Luke 19:46)

Jesus here recalls a crucial passage in which Jeremiah declared the end of God's protection as warrior on behalf of Judah. Responding to the prophets who were prophesying falsely that God would protect Jerusalem and the Temple against
Assyria, Jeremiah answered:

> Will you steal, murder, commit adultery, swear false-
> ly, make offerings to Baal, and go after other gods
> that you have not known, and then come and stand
> before me in this house, which is called by my name,
> and say, "We are safe!"—only to go on doing all these
> abominations? Has this house, which is called by my
> name, become a den of robbers in your sight? . . .
> "Because you have done all these things . . . I will
> cast you out of my sight." (Jeremiah 7:9-11, 13a, 15,
> NRSV)

God went on to instruct the prophet, "As for you, do not pray for this people . . . and do not intercede with me, for I will not hear you" (Jeremiah 7:16, NRSV). Jeremiah was saying: Do not even to pray for God to appear as warrior on behalf of Jerusalem; because of the unfaithfulness of the people, the covenant has been broken.

It was appropriate for Jesus to recall this disastrous prophecy of Jeremiah at the same time that he acted out Zechariah's great prophecy of the return of the king because Zechariah concluded with the proclamation, "there shall be no traders in the house of the Lord of hosts on that day" (Zechariah 14:21b, NRSV). Jesus proclaimed in his actions and words that the kingdom of God was "at hand." By "cleansing the Temple" of money changers, Jesus symbolically reversed the conditions that led Jeremiah to declare doom on Judah; he invited God to act again as warrior on behalf of the people of God against their enemies. Even though Jesus' signs may be obscure to us, their significance was not lost on the religious and civil authorities who understood the threat and "kept looking for a way to kill him" (Mark 12:18, NRSV; Luke 19:47).

As the ultimate symbol of fearlessness, Jesus required his followers to take up the cross. (Matthew 10:38; 16:24; Mark 8:34; Luke 9:23) Why the cross? It was the instrument of torture used by the Roman empire for the specific purpose of terrorizing their subject populations and executing rebels. So Jesus made it his own, as if to ask in scorn, "Is this the worst you can do?"

The followers of Jesus boast in the cross (Galatians 6:14):

> for God's foolishness is wiser than human wisdom, and God's weakness is stronger than human strength. (1 Corinthians 1:25, NRSV)

The message of the cross is unmistakable: we are not to be afraid of the might of empire; indeed, we are to rebel against it. Immanuel is here!

Jesus' rebellion was not just against Rome but against empire itself. In the face of empire, Jesus sent his disciples out to announce, "The kingdom of God is at hand" (Mark 1:15, NAS; Matthew 3:2; 4:17; 10:7; Luke 10:9). Accordingly, the followers of Immanuel take up the cross rather than the sword, because the goal is the kingdom of God on earth as it is in heaven, and that kingdom can only be established when the warfare is God's alone.

In the Book of Isaiah there is a song about the reign of God in which "the sentinels" sing for joy because, "in plain sight they see the return of the Lord to Zion" (v. 8):

> How beautiful upon the mountains
>   are the feet of the messenger who announces
>     peace,
> who brings good news,
>   who announces salvation
>   who says to Zion, "Your God reigns."
> (Isaiah 52:7, NRSV)

When Jesus proclaims that the kingdom of God is at hand, he is announcing, "Your God reigns."

Isaiah is the preeminent prophet to connect the reign of God with the vision of the whole world at peace. In this passage peace comes because God's instruction goes out from Zion.

> In days to come the mountain of the Lord's house
>   shall be established as the highest of the
>     mountains,
>   and shall be raised above the hills;
>   all the nations shall stream to it.

Many peoples shall come and say,
"Come, let us go up to the mountain of the Lord,
  to the house of the God of Jacob;
that he may teach us his ways
  and that we may walk in his paths."

For out of Zion shall go forth instruction,
  and the word of the Lord from Jerusalem.
He shall judge between the nations,
  and shall arbitrate for many peoples;
they shall beat their swords into plowshares,
  and their spears into pruning hooks;
nation shall not lift up sword against nation,
  neither shall they learn war any more.
        (Isaiah 2:1-4, NRSV; Micah 4:1-4)[11]

Jesus, who is Immanuel, who is the Word of God come to dwell among us, who inaugurates the new covenant promise of the law written on the heart so that "they all shall know me," fulfills this vision. In him, instruction goes out of Zion. The community that Jesus instructs will, necessarily, be a peaceable community—a community that bears the fruit of love—because that is a sign of the salvation that he brings:

I have called you friends, because I have made known to you everything that I have heard from my Father. You did not choose me but I chose you. And I appointed you to go and bear fruit, fruit that will last, so that the Father will give you whatever you ask him in my name. I am giving you these commands so that you may love one another. (John 15:15b-17, NRSV)

Instead of war (at least the human warfare of swords, hatred and destruction) Jesus instructs his followers in what it means to the be the children of God:

"You have heard that it was said, 'You shall love your neighbor and hate your enemy.' But I say to you, Love your enemies and pray for those who persecute you, so that you may be children of your Father in heaven; for he makes his sun rise on the evil and on the good, and sends rain on the righteous and on the unrighteous.

For if you love those who love you, what reward do you have? Do not even the tax collectors do the same? And if you greet only your brothers and sisters, what more are you doing than others? Do not even the Gentiles do the same? Be perfect, therefore, as your heavenly Father is perfect. (Matthew 5:43-49, NRSV; Luke 6:27-35)

Here, at last, is the sort of life that only those who live under the protection of the heavenly host can live—just the sort of life that was foreshadowed in the feast by which Elisha turned the armies of the king of Aram from enemies into friends.

This was, of course, Jesus' own holy-war strategy. He healed the servant of the centurion officer (Matthew 8:5-13). He sought out and dined with the collaborationist tax collectors. He even dined with Peter after Peter had betrayed him, and restored him—as he had the others—to that ever-expanding circle of his friends.[12] (John 21:12ff).

The Apostle Paul understood the dynamics of Immanuel's spiritual warfare better than most. So he wrote to the little band of Christians living in the heart of the empire:

Bless those who persecute you; bless and do not curse them. Rejoice with those who rejoice, weep with those who weep. Live in harmony with one another; do not be haughty, but associate with the lowly; do not claim to be wiser than you are. Do not repay anyone evil for evil, but take thought for what is noble in the sight of all. If it is possible, so far as it depends on you, live peaceably with all.

Beloved, never avenge yourselves, but leave room for the wrath of God; for it is written, "Vengeance is mine, I will repay, says the Lord." No, "if your enemies are hungry, feed them; if they are thirsty, give them something to drink; for by doing this you will heap burning coals on their heads." Do not be overcome by evil, but overcome evil with good. (Romans 12:14-21, NRSV)

This combination of practical love of enemies while "leaving room" for God's vengeance sounds jarring to those who do not understand the dynamics of spiritual warfare. But an attitude of vengeance would only lead to bitterness and idolatrous rejection of God. Submission to the evil of oppression would only invite more oppression. Because this is not just a human endeavor, but is the fruit of the spirit of God, the life that Paul teaches in this way combines grace and truth.

In his Letter to the Corinthians, Paul explains:

For though we live in the world, we do not wage war as the world does. The weapons we fight with are not the weapons of the world. On the contrary, they have divine power to demolish strongholds. We demolish arguments and every pretension that sets itself up against the knowledge of God, and we take captive every thought to make it obedient to Christ. (2 Corinthians 10:3-5, NIV)

Because Paul saw the spiritual warfare of the people of God in these terms, when he wrote to the Christians in Rome, the overarching instruction was,

> Do not be conformed to this world, but be trans-
> formed by the renewing of your minds, so that you
> may discern what is the will of God—what is good
> and acceptable and perfect. (Romans 12:2, NRSV)

This is a warning to those who dwell in the heart of the empire
not to let their minds be held captive by the assumptions of
the culture that surrounds them. Instead, Paul points them
to the promise of the new covenant and to Eden, where God
alone decides what is good and what is evil.

For Paul, the essence of the problem is that "the god of this
world has blinded the minds of the unbelievers." (2 Corinthians 4:4, NRSV) Ultimately, the enemy is not the Emperor or
his agents, nor their soldiers with their oppressive taxes. Nor is
the enemy the elite among the collaborationists who "join field
to field" and "grind the face of the poor." Nor is the enemy the
slave holder, or the abusive husband. These are merely several
among the many ways in which sin's destructive power is revealed. Although any of these may legitimately be recognized
as "enemies," in truth they are just people whose minds have
been blinded by "the god of this world."

The enemy, the *real* enemy, is the Evil One who blinds the
mind, who hardens the heart, and thus deprives us of communion with God.

> For our struggle is not against enemies of blood and
> flesh, but against the rulers, against the authorities,
> against the cosmic powers of this present darkness,
> against the spiritual forces of evil in the heavenly
> places.
>
> Therefore take up the whole armor of God, so that
> you may be able to withstand on that evil day, and
> having done everything, to stand firm. Stand there-

fore, and fasten the belt of truth around your waist, and put on the breastplate of righteousness. As shoes for your feet put on whatever will make you ready to proclaim the gospel of peace. With all of these, take the shield of faith, with which you will be able to quench all the flaming arrows of the evil one. Take the helmet of salvation, and the sword of the Spirit, which is the word of God. (Ephesians 6:12-17, NRSV; cf., Isaiah 59:15-18)

Because the real enemy is the loss of communion with God, the only weapon that can be effective in this battle is the "sword of the Spirit, which is the word of God." For the rest, the task is to stand firm and be unafraid, to live in the confidence that "perfect love that casts out fear." Following the lead of Jesus, we strengthen our resolve by taking symbolic actions that reassert the humanity of the oppressed, and join together in the community of those who are learning to love one another because they themselves have experienced the loving presence of God (1 John 4:7-21). As such, the life of the community itself becomes a prophetic sign of Immanuel as we await with confidence the appearance of Yahweh *sabaot*.

### *The War of the Lamb*

The spiritual war of the Lamb is the primary theme of the Revelation of John. In his vision, John sees that the oppressive forces of the world

will make war on the Lamb, and the Lamb will conquer them, for he is Lord of lords and King of kings, and those with him are called and chosen and faithful. (Revelation 17:14, NRSV)

The Lamb, of course, is Jesus Christ, who was named "the Lamb of God who takes away the sin of the world" in the Gospel of John (John 1:29, NRSV). Ultimately, the Lamb will triumph because he is also the Word of God (John 1:14). The vision of the final battle emphasizes that the weapon of his victory is the "sword" from his mouth, which is, of course, not a physical sword, but the Word:

> Then I saw heaven opened, and there was a white horse! Its rider is called Faithful and True, and in righteousness he judges and makes war. His eyes are like a flame of fire, and on his head are many diadems; and he has a name inscribed that no one knows but himself. He is clothed in a robe dipped in blood, and his name is called The Word of God. And the armies of heaven, wearing fine linen, white and pure, were following him on white horses. From his mouth comes a sharp sword with which to strike down the nations . . . .

> Then I saw the beast and the kings of the earth with their armies gathered to make war against the rider on the horse and against his army. And the beast was captured, and with it the false prophet who had performed in its presence the signs by which he deceived those who had received the mark of the beast and those who worshiped its image. These two were thrown alive into the lake of fire that burns with sulfur. And the rest were killed by the sword of the rider on the horse, the sword that came from his mouth . . . . (Revelation 19:11-21, NRSV; cf., Isaiah 63:1-6)

The war of the Lamb, then, is a symbolic way of speaking about the spiritual process by which the word of God goes out into the world bringing salvation. It is, in a sense, what this whole study is about. It is the process by which people who have become captives of Mystery Babylon are rescued from the false gods Molech and *mammon* and brought into the community of grace and truth. It is that painful inward and spiritual journey through which people humble themselves and exchange their independent judgments of good and evil for God's. The war of the Lamb is the operation by which God takes hearts of stone and turns them into hearts of flesh.

This brings us to the final point to be made about the spiritual war of the Lamb. That has to do with suffering. There is a crucial relationship between the acceptance of suffering and the growth of mercy. This is the deepest significance of the incarnation:

> It was fitting that God, for whom and through whom all things exist, in bringing many children to glory, should make the pioneer of their salvation perfect through sufferings. . . . [Jesus] had to become like his brothers and sisters in every respect, so that he might be a merciful and faithful high priest in the service of God, to make a sacrifice of atonement for the sins of the people. Because he himself was tested by what he suffered, he is able to help those who are being tested. (Hebrews 2:10, 17-18, NRSV)

In the end, the final victory of the Lamb is predicated upon the willingness of the Lamb to suffer death on the cross (Revelation 5:9-12). This is so intrinsic to his victory that he is called, "the Lamb that was slain from the foundation of the world" (Revelation 15:8, KJV).

The Lamb conquers in the company of those with him, "the chosen and faithful" (Revelation 17:14, NRSV)—and they must share in the essential character of their Lord. As the Lamb is victorious through his suffering and through the sword of the Word, so also the saints of God. In Chapter 12 of his Revelation, John sees a vision of "war in heaven" and of the victory of God's people:

> Then I heard a loud voice in heaven, proclaiming,
>
> "Now have come the salvation and the power
>   and the kingdom of our God
>   and the authority of his Messiah,
> for the accuser of our comrades has been thrown
>     down,
>   who accuses them day and night before our God.
> But they have conquered him by the blood of the
>     Lamb
>   and by the word of their testimony,
>   for they did not cling to life even in the face of
>     death."
>
> (Revelation 12:10-11, NRSV)

The peaceable community of God conquers by "the blood of the Lamb and by the word of their testimony." In Greek, "testimony" is the word *martyrias* from which the English word "martyr" is derived. It is the same word that Jesus used when he appeared to the disciples after his crucifixion and told them:

> But you will receive power when the Holy Spirit has come upon you; and you will be my witnesses/*martyres* in Jerusalem, in all Judea and Samaria, and to the ends of the earth." (Acts 1:8, NRSV)

Martyr is an appropriate word because the spiritual war of the Lamb to which it points is still a war, for all that it is spiritual. The powers of the world are, perhaps, more aware of the threat posed to their dominion by the testimony that Jesus is the Lamb of God than are even the people of God. Jesus forewarned his disciples of this at the last supper:

> "If the world hates you, be aware that it hated me before it hated you. If you belonged to the world, the world would love you as its own. Because you do not belong to the world, but I have chosen you out of the world—therefore the world hates you. Remember the word that I said to you, 'Servants are not greater than their master.' If they persecuted me, they will persecute you. . . . " (John 15:18-20a, NRSV; cf., Matthew 10:24-25)

Neither Jesus nor his followers sought suffering, nor did Jesus teach that suffering is somehow good in itself. Jesus was, however, clear that his way was in conflict with the culture of the world. Bearing witness, being "martyrs," may or may not require physical death, but it does mean not clinging to life. Being a witness/*martus* is incompatible with worldly power. Since God's salvation reaches beyond death, Jesus' followers can stand firm even in the face of suffering because they know, experientially, that the new heaven and new earth are coming.

Paul told the Corinthian church that "God, who reconciled us to himself through Christ, . . . has given us the ministry of reconciliation" (2 Corinthians 5:18, NRSV). Then he showed them what that ministry looked like in his own life:

> as servants of God we have commended ourselves in every way: through great endurance, in afflictions, hardships, calamities, beatings, imprisonments, riots, labors, sleepless nights, hunger; by purity, knowledge, patience, kindness, holiness of spirit, genuine love, truthful speech, and the power of God; with the weapons of righteousness for the right hand and for the left; in honor and dishonor, in ill repute and good repute. We are treated as impostors, and yet are true; as unknown, and yet are well known; as dying, and see—we are alive; as punished, and yet not

killed; as sorrowful, yet always rejoicing; as poor, yet making many rich; as having nothing, and yet possessing everything. (2 Corinthians 6:4-10, NRSV)

This is a general rule of faith. The instruction of Jesus that any who wished to follow him must take up their cross daily is more than a prophetic sign of the fearlessness of the people of God; it is the way in which the spiritual war of the Lamb is waged in this world, until the end of the age. It is, in fact, by willingly accepting suffering for truth that disciples become joint heirs with Christ:

> For all who are led by the Spirit of God are children of God. For you did not receive a spirit of slavery to fall back into fear, but you have received a spirit of adoption. When we cry, "Abba! Father!" it is that very Spirit bearing witness with our spirit that we are children of God, and if children, then heirs, heirs of God and joint heirs with Christ—*if, in fact, we suffer with him so that we may also be glorified with him.* (Romans 8:14-17, NRSV, my emphasis; cf., Colossians 1:24; Philippians 3:10-11)

"Abba! Father!" was Jesus' cry at Gesthemene the night before he was arrested. It is the cry of anyone who is afraid but nevertheless is willing to say to God, "Yet not what I will, but what you will" (Mark 14:36, NIV; Matthew 26:39; Luke 22:42).

Ultimately, that prayer is the basis of our salvation. On the faith that God does indeed know better than we what is good and what is evil, we rest our hope. It is on that basis that the peaceable people of God receive their blessing:

"Blessed are the peacemakers,
  for they will be called children of God.
Blessed are those who are persecuted for
  righteousness' sake,
  for theirs is the kingdom of heaven.
Blessed are you when people revile you and
    persecute you and utter all kinds of evil against
    you falsely on my account.
  Rejoice and be glad, for your reward is great in
  heaven. . . ."
(Matthew 5:9-12a, NRSV)

In the end, the suffering and peaceable community of the people of God rely upon the truth that Immanuel, the Lamb of God, can and will be victorious, and that they will share in that victory:

"Blessed are the meek,
  for they will inherit the earth."
(Matthew 5:5, NRSV)

The community that chooses to live by Jesus' way of cross, is a sign of salvation.

---

[1] "Holy war" is, in fact, not a biblical term. It was coined much later in the state church era of Christianity. I am, however, using the term as descriptive of a strand of the scriptural tradition sometimes called "divine warfare" or "Yahweh war" that includes legislation concerning the involvement of the people of God in warfare (e.g., Deuteronomy 20), as well as those narratives in which God is portrayed as actively involved in instigating or carrying out warfare.

² Incidentally, I think that the laws of holy warfare in Deuteronomy make the best biblical case against military conscription
even for those Christians or Jews who are not pacifists.

³ The Hebrew text at verse 6 has proven difficult for the translators. There is textual support for a reading followed by most
versions to say that the "lappers" used their hands (presumably
unlike dogs) and they were chosen. (This then allows for the
interpretation that the 300 were the elite soldiers.) I prefer the
NRSV version because I've never seen a dog kneel—dogs drink
standing on all fours—and the selection of the foolish soldiers
seems to me more consistent with the story. In either case, the
main point remains: God reduced the human power of Gideon's
army so that it would be clear that God, not the army, saved Israel
from the Mideanites.

⁴ The end of King David's life was tragic. He ordered a census
(indicating his increasing reliance upon human calculation and
military power). The divine punishment that it merited closes 2
Samuel 24 and brings the story of David to an end. How far he
had fallen from his original simple faith.

⁵ See Jeremiah 19:5 and 2 Kings 23:10.

⁶ 2 Kings 17 records the end of the Kingdom of Israel with
the conquest of Samaria by Sargon II of Assyria in 721 B.C. The
catalog of the sins of the kings of Israel includes passing their
sons and daughters through fire, making golden calves, etc., and
(perhaps decisively) an attempted military alliance with Egypt
against Assyria (2 Kings 17:4). The prophet Hosea, about this
time, recalled the words of Samuel in his own prophecy:

I will destroy you, O Israel; who can help you? Where now
is your king, that he may save you? Where in all your cities
are your rulers, of whom you said, "Give me a king and rulers?" I gave you a king in my anger, and I took him away in
my wrath. (Hosea 13:9-11, NRSV)

In 587 B.C., when Judah fell, Jeremiah charged Judah with
having changed gods and "dug cisterns that do not hold water"
(Jeremiah 2:11-13, NRSV). In addition to the oppression of the
poor (see v. 34), those cisterns were military alliances contracted
between Judah and Egypt and Assyria (see v. 18) against Nebuchadnezzar of Babylon.

⁷ After Jesus' birth, Simeon prophesies to Mary, "This child is destined for the falling and the rising of many in Israel, and to be a sign that will be opposed" (Luke 2:34, NRSV). The sign of Immanuel is inevitably ambiguous; it carries hope for the obedient; destruction for the faithless.

⁸ The scripture quotation that Jesus used in this encounter with Satan, Deuteronomy 6:12-13, is introduced in a passage concerning Yahweh's triumph when he rescued the people "out of the land of Egypt, out of the house of slavery" and brought Israel into the land of plenty. Jesus selected this affirmation of the sole worship of God precisely because it contains the historically demonstrated power of God to overcome the power of the nations.

⁹ Recall the argument, page 67ff that in the new covenant the kingdom of God would necessarily be a voluntary community. This change in the social structure of the kingdom of God (from ethnic and geographic to voluntary) requires a corollary shift in the nature of the holy war. No longer can humans join in God's warfare, for that would contradict the interiority of the new covenant promises upon which the community is based.

¹⁰ See, especially, Walter Wink, "Jesus' Third Way: Nonviolent Engagement," in *Engaging the Powers*, Minneapolis, MN: Fortress Press, 1992, 175-193. Wink convincingly interprets these verses as Jesus' instruction in nonviolent resistance: an inferior who has been slapped asserts his humanity by requiring the opponent to hit him as an equal; a peasant gets a soldier who has conscripted his help into trouble by exceeding the legal authority of conscription; a victim of a lawsuit embarrasses the court by going naked thus putting the prosecutor in the wrong.

¹¹ In an interesting switch on this imagery, in Joel 3:9-16, Yahweh summons the nations to the final battle, telling them, "beat your plowshares into swords ..." The prophets thus put a pointed question: Who do you want to be, the faithless nations called to arm themselves or the peaceable community of God called to disarm themselves because Yahweh, himself, will judge between the nations?

[12] In the list of the twelve disciples in Luke there is one "Simon, who was called the Zealot" (Luke 6:15, NRSV) but who is called "the Cananean" in the other Gospels. Whether or not his name indicates that he was a recruit from the violent revolutionaries later called "Zealots" is disputed. The name "Judas Iscariot" is also intriguing. While it may simply reflect the name of his home town, there is a similarity with the name of the daggers used for political assassination of Roman collaborators: the *sicarii*. While the prior political identities of this Simon and Judas will never be known, my guess is that Jesus' strategy for extending the kingdom of God included recruiting from the violent rebellion, just as it included recruiting disciples like "Matthew, the tax collector" from the world of the collaborationists.

# THE SIGN OF THE COMMUNITY
## OF GRACE AND TRUTH

*I*t is the inclusive, bountiful, and peaceable community, formed by listening to the *qol Yahweh*, that will celebrate the marriage feast of the Lamb. Jesus tells this parable:

"The kingdom of heaven may be compared to a king who gave a wedding banquet for his son. He sent his slaves to call those who had been invited to the wedding banquet, but they would not come.

Again he sent other slaves, saying, 'Tell those who have been invited: Look, I have prepared my dinner, my oxen and my fat calves have been slaughtered, and everything is ready; come to the wedding banquet.'

But they made light of it and went away, one to his farm, another to his business, while the rest seized his slaves, mistreated them, and killed them. The king was enraged. He sent his troops, destroyed those murderers, and burned their city.

Then he said to his slaves, 'The wedding is ready, but those invited were not worthy. Go therefore into the main streets, and invite everyone you find to the wedding banquet.' Those slaves went out into the streets and gathered all whom they found, both good and bad; so the wedding hall was filled with guests." (Matthew 22:2-10, NRSV)

Those for whom the banquet had been prepared were declared "not worthy" because of their greediness and violence. As in the other parable of the banquet, God invites everyone: the kingdom of heaven is the inclusive community of all those who choose to respond to the invitation.

Jesus ends this parable with a surprising twist:

"But when the king came in to see the guests, he noticed a man there who was not wearing a wedding robe, and he said to him, 'Friend, how did you get in here without a wedding robe?' And he was speechless." (Matthew 22:11-12, NRSV)

At first hearing, it seems unfair that the king should question someone who was pulled off the streets unexpectedly for failing to have on wedding robes. However, in telling this story, Jesus is drawing on the passage from Isaiah with which he began his public ministry:

The spirit of the Lord God is upon me, because the Lord has anointed me; he has sent me to bring good news to the oppressed. . . . He has clothed me with the garments of salvation, he has covered me with the robe of righteousness, as a bridegroom decks himself with a garland, and as a bride adorns herself with her jewels. (Isaiah 61:1, 10, NRSV; Luke 4:18; c.f., Psalm 132:9, 16; Revelation 19:8)

The wedding robe stands for righteousness, which is a gift from God. These are "the garments of salvation." In Jesus' parable of the wedding banquet, the Lord of the banquet gave all the guests (good and bad), who were pulled in off the roadways, wedding robes as they came in to the celebration. It appears that only this guest had refused the gift of righteousness. And so Jesus brings his story to an end:

> Then the king said to the attendants, 'Bind him hand and foot, and throw him into the outer darkness, where there will be weeping and gnashing of teeth.' (Matthew 22:13, NRSV)

Jesus finds room for God's judgment even in this parable of overwhelming grace.

Jesus' parable points to an amazing tension in the life of the new covenant community. The community is made up of those who have allowed God to write the law of righteousness on their hearts. Since participation in the community of salvation is voluntary under the new covenant, it is also possible, at any time, for an individual to reject the inward teaching of the Holy Spirit. The community betrays the essence of the Gospel if, in its urge to inclusivity, it attempts to include within itself members who willfully reject the gift of the law written on their hearts. The new covenant community must be a sign of the power of the cross to bring righteousness from God into the world.

This means that the community of salvation has to face the question of discipline and accountability. At the same time, the community must retain the blessing of forgiveness, which is of the essence of Jesus' role as mediator of the new covenant. In short, the community must reflect both God's grace and God's truth.

Jesus teaches about this in Matthew 18. He begins by telling the parable of the shepherd who left the ninety-nine sheep to save the one who was lost. Having thus struck the note of gracious inclusiveness, he goes on to make a practical application of the parable:

> "If another member of the church sins against you, go and point out the fault when the two of you are alone. If the member listens to you, you have regained that one." (Matthew 18:15, NRSV)

Sometimes the task is not easy, so Jesus adds:

> "But if you are not listened to, take one or two others along with you, so that every word may be confirmed by the evidence of two or three witnesses." (Matthew 18:16, NRSV)

These steps safeguard the dignity of all involved. The life of the community depends on the willingness of all its members to walk in humility in mutual submission. Misunderstandings and hurt melt before the mutual search for truth and the common good. But sometimes, for whatever reason, some persist in their offense. Still, the community as a whole labors to extend love and restore unity:

> "If the member refuses to listen to them, tell it to the church; and if the offender refuses to listen even to the church, let such a one be to you as a Gentile and a tax collector." (Matthew 18:17, NRSV)

This drastic step comes only when the offender is obstinate; it is the final safeguard of the character of the church as witness to the power of Christ for salvation. The judgment of the church does not carry power over the eternal destiny of the individual (the final judgment remains God's), and it does not even imply that the individual is to be shunned. After all, with whom did Jesus like better to dine than with tax collectors and sinners? In this instruction, Jesus simply calls for the community to clearly state that the individual is out of unity with the truth of God as the community knows it. This functions as a definitive warning to those within the community of faith and those outside not to be deceived: we believe that this individual still stands in need of the Great Physician—even if he or she is not ready to admit that fact.

Having laid out the process of careful laboring within the church, Jesus explains the authority of the church to exercise discipline.

> "Truly I tell you, whatever you [plural] bind on earth will be bound in heaven, and whatever you [plural] loose on earth will be loosed in heaven.

> "Again, truly I tell you, if two of you agree on earth about anything you ask, it will be done for you by my Father in heaven. For where two or three are gathered in my name, I am there among them." (Matthew 18:18-20, NRSV)

The key to discipline within the church is the living presence of Christ. Discipline, inevitably, involves judgment about whether particular behaviors are right or wrong. Indeed, if the church's life is to be a sign of salvation, it must make "right judgment" (John 7:24, NIV). But this is dangerous ground, for the entire basis of the life of the community of salvation is that it has yielded the judgment of good and evil to God alone.

Therefore, it is great good news, and no accident, that Jesus' promise to be present in the midst of the community of faith comes precisely in the context of the exercise of discipline. Only the qualities of grace and truth that Jesus uniquely brings together can overcome the power of sin in people's lives. When Jesus speaks of giving the church the power to bind and loose, he is conferring nothing less than the ability to bring this same combination of grace and truth into people's lives.

### The Mystery of Binding and Loosing

When Jesus asked his disciples who they thought he was, "Simon Peter answered, 'You are the Christ, the Son of the living God'" (Matthew 16:16, NIV). This answer provoked Jesus' most profound teaching about the authority of the community of believers:

> And Jesus answered him, "Blessed are you, Simon son of Jonah! For flesh and blood has not revealed this to you, but my Father in heaven. And I tell you, you are Peter, and on this rock I will build my church. (Matthew 16:17-18a, NRSV)

Peter's confession, "Jesus is the Christ, the son of the living God," is the rock upon which the kingdom of God is built.

The rock that Jesus had in mind was not bedrock, but the multitude of relatively little rocks with which the Holy Land is littered. Those rocks are good for throwing, as has been proved during a thousand insurrections, so Jesus goes on to say of the church, "and the gates of Hades will not prevail against it." (Matthew 15:18b, NRSV) The confession of faith in Jesus as the Christ is an effective weapon for extending the kingdom of God. It is the sword of the mouth in the vision of the Book of Revelation 19:15. With every additional soul and body liberated from the power of death, territory has been seized from the Evil One. People have been released from the curse occasioned by sin and carried through the flaming sword (Genesis

3:24), back into Paradise. This is how Jesus understands the ministry of the church.

Continuing his dialogue with Simon Peter, Jesus went on to say more about the authority of this ministry:

> I will give you the keys of the kingdom of heaven, and whatever you bind on earth will be bound in heaven, and whatever you loose on earth will be loosed in heaven." (Matthew 16:19, NRSV)[1]

These words, "binding" and "loosing," appeared frequently in Jesus' ministry. A dispute arose after Jesus had healed a man who was blind and mute, and the Pharisees said, "'It is only by the Beelzebul, the ruler of the demons, that this fellow casts out the demons.'" (Matthew 12:24, NRSV) Jesus answered:

> "And if Satan casts out Satan, he is divided against himself; how then shall his kingdom stand? And if I by Beelzebul cast out demons, by whom do your sons cast them out? Consequently they shall be your judges. But if I cast out demons by the Spirit of God, then the kingdom of God has come upon you. Or how can anyone enter the strong man's house and carry off his property, unless he first binds the strong man? And then he will plunder his house." (Matthew 12:26-29, NAS)

Jesus sums up his ministry of overcoming demonic forces with the figure of binding the strong man. In its ministries of healing and forgiveness, the church is plundering the dominion of Satan.

On another occasion—it was a Sabbath day—Jesus healed a woman who had been crippled for eighteen years. This caused an uproar because a leader in the synagogue thought Jesus was violating the Sabbath commandment.

> But the Lord answered him and said, "You hypocrites! Does not each of you on the sabbath untie his ox or his donkey from the manger, and lead it away to give it water? And ought not this woman, a daughter of Abraham whom Satan bound for eighteen long years, be set free from this bondage on the sabbath day?" (Luke 13:15-16, NRSV)

The Bible goes on to say that the people "were rejoicing" because God was powerfully at work in their midst.

These examples show Jesus' understanding of his ministry of healing. When he healed the blind and mute man, Jesus saw himself as "binding" Satan. When he healed the crippled woman, Jesus saw himself as "loosing" a woman who had been "bound" by Satan. When Jesus told Peter that he was giving him the power to bind and to loose, he was giving the church the authority to carry on his work of healing and setting people free from bondage.

This is the same authority Jesus gave to the twelve and then the seventy-two when he sent them out to proclaim the kingdom of God and "gave them power and authority over all demons and to cure diseases" (Luke 9:1, NRSV; c.f., 10:9). Jesus saw his disciples going out, proclaiming that the kingdom of God is at hand, raising an assault on the kingdom of Satan. When the seventy-two returned and reported on all they had done, Jesus replied, "I watched Satan fall from heaven like a flash of lightning" (Luke 10:18, NRSV).

There is a close relationship between the authority to heal and the authority to forgive sin. When his friends brought the paralytic to Jesus to be healed, Jesus responded by forgiving sin. To those who questioned his authority to do this, he responded by giving them evidence of physical healing:

"For which is easier, to say, 'Your sins are forgiven,' or to say, 'Stand up and walk'? But so that you may know that the Son of Man has authority on earth to forgive sins"—he then said to the paralytic—"Stand up, take your bed and go to your home." (Matthew 9:5-6, NRSV; c.f. Mark 2:9-11; Luke 5:23-24; see also Psalm 103:2-3)

When Jesus gave the church the authority to bind and loose in the context of the discipline of a member of the community who persists in an offense, he was still talking about the power of God to heal. Physical healing and the forgiveness of sin both bind the Evil One, and set people free to live the life God intended from the beginning of creation.

### The Countersign of Discipline

Sinful behaviors are an expression of bondage to Satan and death; to free a person from bondage, in whatever form it takes, is to restore her or him to paradise. "If the Son makes you free, you will be free indeed" (John 8:36, NRSV).

In the case of both physical healing and sin, the one who is suffering needs to come to God to be set free. Healing and forgiveness both require recognition that there is a problem. Discipline within the community of believers has to do with helping a friend come to an awareness that he or she is calling "good" what God is calling "evil." For the Evil One to be bound, there must be truth speaking as well as grace.

An example of this sort of discipline occurs in Paul's correspondence with the community of believers at Corinth. It concerns the case of a man who is having sexual relations with his father's wife. Paul writes to Corinth with a sense of outrage:

> It is actually reported that there is sexual immorality among you, and of a kind that is not found even among pagans; for a man is living with his father's wife. (1 Corinthians 5:1, NRSV)

What really astounds Paul is not the sin itself, but rather that the church has accepted it. The Corinthians have apparently boasted of their spirituality, so Paul writes:

> And you are arrogant! Should you not rather have mourned, so that he who has done this would have been removed from among you? (1 Corinthians 5:2, NRSV)

By its witness of condoning this behavior, Paul says, the church of Corinth is now proclaiming a Gospel that has no power to free people from bondage to sin. Instead, their so-called Gospel separates salvation from righteousness, destroys the unity of flesh and spirit, and empties the cross of its power (See 1 Corinthians 1:17ff).

Paul continues with words of amazing, even horrible, power:

> Even though I am not physically present, I am with you in spirit. And I have already passed judgment on the one who did this, just as if I were present. When you are assembled in the name of our Lord Jesus and I am with you in spirit, and the power of our Lord Jesus is present, hand this man over to Satan, so that the sinful nature may be destroyed and his spirit saved on the day of the Lord. (1 Corinthians 5:3-5, NIV)

Elsewhere, Paul wrote, "[God] has rescued us from the power of darkness and transferred us into the kingdom of his beloved Son" (Colossians 1:13, NRSV). When he uses the phrase, "hand this man over to Satan," he is reversing this imagery. Paul has simply found another metaphor for Jesus' instruction that the church must treat the one who refuses to listen to the church as a Gentile or tax collector.

Sometimes it is necessary for those who love a person who has fallen into deeply self-destructive behavior to intervene in his or her situation in drastic ways. To continue life together as usual, would imply that all is well. By refusing to cooperate in this person's destructive lifestyle, they hope to so disrupt the destructive patterns that she or he will be willing to seek health and restoration. Paul calls for a drastic intervention in the hope that the offender may yet be saved.

In his correspondence with the Corinthian church, Paul at one point refers to an earlier letter about someone who has since been punished by the church:

> For I wrote you out of much distress and anguish of heart and with many tears, not to cause you pain, but to let you know the abundant love that I have for you. But if anyone has caused pain, he has caused it not to me, but to some extent—not to exaggerate it—to all of you. This punishment by the majority is enough for such a person; so now instead you should forgive and console him, so that he may not be overwhelmed by excessive sorrow. So I urge you to reaffirm your love for him.

> I wrote for this reason: to test you and to know whether you are obedient in everything. Anyone whom you forgive, I also forgive. What I have forgiven, if I have forgiven anything, has been for your sake in the presence of Christ. And we do this so that we may not be outwitted by Satan; for we are not ignorant of his designs. (2 Corinthians 2:4-11, NRSV)

Is this the same man who was found living with his father's wife? It is impossible to know. If the two are the same, the story serves as a beautiful demonstration of restoration being realized. God's design is to embrace all people in the community of salvation, which is also the community of righteousness. Satan's design is to use judgment to bring about their exclusion. The tools of discipline that the community of faith has at its disposal are the presence of Christ, the power of binding and loosing, the word of forgiveness. This is the power of the sword of the Word.

We need to look even more closely at the relationship between truth and grace in the formation of the community of faith. The sexual laws in Leviticus are initially given in Chapter 18 and repeated in Chapter 20 where the death penalty is decreed for their violation. In between—in Chapter 19—are a remarkable series of laws concerning justice and God's inclusive love:

> You shall love your neighbor as yourself . . . (Leviticus 19:18, NRSV)

and

> The alien who resides with you shall be to you as the citizen among you; you shall love the alien as yourself, for you were aliens in the land of Egypt: I am the Lord your God. (Leviticus 19:34, NRSV; cf., Numbers 15:16)

Jesus referred to these laws of love when he answered the question about which commandments were the greatest (Matthew 22:36ff) and when, in the parable of the Good Samaritan (Luke 10:25-37), he equated love of neighbor with love of the alien. But Jesus did not neglect the surrounding laws of

206

sexual righteousness found in Leviticus 18 and 20. A prime example occurs in the Sermon on the Mount in the passage in which Jesus extended the law against adultery from gross acts of the flesh to the heart:

> "You have heard that it was said, 'You shall not commit adultery.' But I say to you that everyone who looks at a woman with lust has already committed adultery with her in his heart. (Matthew 5:27-28, NRSV)

Clearly, Jesus saw that justice and sexual purity were both crucial building blocks for community—and were matters of concern to the kingdom of God.

But when it came to judgment, Jesus changed the law—or, it would perhaps be more accurate to say, he *fulfilled* the law. When the woman who was caught *in* adultery was brought to him (John 8:1-11), he did not demand that the woman (or the man—who must have been caught with her, if she was indeed "caught in adultery") be brought out and stoned as both Leviticus 20:10 and Deuteronomy 22:22 demand. Instead, Jesus said to her—as he says to all:

> "Neither do I condemn you. Go your way, and from now on do not sin again." (John 8:11b, NRSV)

As to the woman caught in adultery, so to the man in Corinth who had sex with his father's wife. In Leviticus, God has given this instruction:

> The man who lies with his father's wife has uncovered his father's nakedness; both of them shall be put to death; their blood is upon them. (Leviticus 20:11, NRSV)

Within Judaism in the period just before Jesus lived, there was a horror of sexual sin. In *Jubilees*, a book certainly known by New Testament authors including Paul, lying with one's father's wife is described as unforgivable:

> there is no forgiveness in order to atone for a man who has done this, forever. . . . (Jubilees 33:13)[2]

In contrast to the church that decrees that for this or that sinful behavior "there is no forgiveness . . . forever," Jesus proclaims only one "unforgivable sin."

One day he was carrying on his ministry of healing, and "when his family heard it, they went out to restrain him," thinking him to be crazed (Mark 3:21, NRSV). Religious leaders also came down to challenge what he was doing. This was the setting of his explanation, already mentioned, that in healing people he was "binding the strong man." He then went on to say:

> "Truly I tell you, people will be forgiven for their sins and whatever blasphemies they utter; but whoever blasphemes against the Holy Spirit can never have forgiveness, but is guilty of an eternal sin" (Mark 3:28-29, NRSV)

The one thing unforgivable is to deny the healing presence and power of the Holy Spirit.[3] It is only "unforgivable" in the sense that God cannot forgive when the offender refuses to acknowledge the reality of a living God. God has chosen, in love, to respect human freedom and not to force his forgiveness on anyone.

After he spoke these words about unforgivable sin, the crowd told Jesus that his family was there looking for him.

> And he replied, "Who are my mother and my broth-
> ers?" And looking at those who sat around him, he
> said, "Here are my mother and my brothers! Who-
> ever does the will of God is my brother and sister
> and mother." (Mark 3:33-34, NRSV)

Here Jesus reaffirms that the basis of true community is
attention to the living word of God. And as he has just said,
the "finger of God" or God's active presence, is demonstrated
in the work of healing and freeing people from the power of
Satan. The community that denies God's power to bind the
strong man and loose healing and forgiveness on the earth is,
therefore, a false community. Even when it claims to define itself by its adherence to God's laws, or by its right confession of
faith, or even by the sanctity of family (see Matthew 10:34-37;
Luke 14:26), if it uses those things to bring condemnation and
exclusion on others, it is a false community. The naming of sin
in the community of truth and grace must only be in the interest of restoration.

For this reason, Jesus concludes his teaching about discipline within the fellowship of believers (as recorded in Matthew) with this dialogue about forgiveness:

> Then Peter came and said to him, "Lord, if another
> member of the church sins against me, how often
> should I forgive? As many as seven times?"
>
> Jesus said to him, "Not seven times, but, I tell you,
> seventy-seven times. (Matthew 18:21-22, NRSV)

As with the parable of the lost sheep that opened this teaching, the principle is the same: God is determined that everyone
who is willing should be saved.

Jesus made a point of welcoming the most vulnerable and wounded into the circle of his particular friends. Jesus was dining with a Pharisee when a woman "who was a sinner" came in and washed Jesus' feet with her tears, dried them with her hair, and poured perfume on them. This created an uproar, but Jesus said this:

> "Therefore, I tell you, her sins, which were many, have been forgiven; hence she has shown great love. But the one to whom little is forgiven, loves little." Then he said to her, "Your sins are forgiven."

Those who were at the table with him began to say among themselves, "Who is this who even forgives sins?" but Jesus said to the woman, "Your faith has saved you; go in peace" (Luke 7:47-50, NRSV). The fact is that the church is composed entirely of sinners. When we try to pretend otherwise, we lie and deny the power of God to save. The Apostle John said as much:

> If we say that we have no sin, we deceive ourselves, and the truth is not in us. If we confess our sins, he who is faithful and just will forgive us our sins and cleanse us from all unrighteousness. If we say that we have not sinned, we make him a liar, and his word is not in us. (1 John 1:8-10, NRSV)

There can be no such thing as a church of Jesus Christ that does not welcome a prostitute, an adulterer, a homosexual, a thief or someone addicted to drugs, alcohol, greed or violence. In the Gospel of Luke story about the pious Pharisee and the tax collector, whom did Jesus say "went down to his home justified"? The Pharisee had done his best to follow all the laws of God and had worked himself up to a position of respectability in the church. The tax collector was a collaborator with the occupying military power, a man who venially exploited his fellows to enrich himself.

> "But the tax collector, standing far off, would not even look up to heaven, but was beating his breast and saying, 'God, be merciful to me, a sinner!'
>
> "I tell you, this man went down to his home justified rather than the other; for all who exalt themselves will be humbled, but all who humble themselves will be exalted." (Luke 18:13-14, NRSV)

The pharisaic church reverses these roles. It insists that all who come into the community must pretend that they do not bear the scars of sin from living in this world. In the pharisaic church, if any sin is confessed, it is one that is safely buried in the past. By contrast, the community of salvation is the community of grace and truth, which recognizes sin (whether the private sins of its members or the great social sins of oppression and violence) for the sole—and glorious—purpose of carrying out the power Jesus has given to bind and loose. Let the healing begin!

### Robes Washed in the Blood of the Lamb

The vision of salvation is a vision of the throng of the weak, the poor, and the lonely—and also the arrogant, the oppressor, and the selfish—who have all come to Jesus to be loosed from bondage to Satan. Freed to attend to the voice of the living God, they come into the community of grace and truth. This is the New Jerusalem, and "its gates will never be shut . . . but nothing unclean will enter it. . ." (Revelation 21:25, 27a, NRSV). The community gathers together in joyful celebration around the throne:

and there was a great multitude that no one could count, from every nation, from all tribes and peoples and languages, standing before the throne and before the Lamb, robed in white, with palm branches in their hands. They cried out in a loud voice, saying,

"Salvation belongs to our God who is seated on the throne, and to the Lamb!"

Then one of the elders addressed me, saying, "Who are these, robed in white, and where have they come from?" I said to him, "Sir, you are the one that knows." Then he said to me, "These are they who have come out of the great ordeal; they have washed their robes and made them white in the blood of the Lamb.

For this reason they are before the throne of God, and worship him day and night within his temple, and the one who is seated on the throne will shelter them. They will hunger no more, and thirst no more; the sun will not strike them, nor any scorching heat; for the Lamb at the center of the throne will be their shepherd, and he will guide them to springs of the water of life, and God will wipe away every tear from their eyes." (Revelation 7:9-17, NRSV)

Robed in white, the community of the saved are all sinners who have been touched by Jesus and have come to a place of peace where the truth is spoken in love. Where such communities exist in this world, there is a sign of salvation.

[1] In the context of disciplining an unrepentant sinner, the church has sometimes been tempted to believe that Jesus had it in mind to give the community the authority to utter words of eternal condemnation. In the Gospel of John, we read the words of the resurrected Jesus:

"If you forgive the sins of any, they are forgiven them; if you retain the sins of any, they are retained." (John 20:23, NRSV)

Despite the phrase about retaining sin, Jesus must be speaking to the power to forgive; it seems impossible that he would confer an authority to condemn, for in the same Gospel he denies that his ministry is to bring any to condemnation:

I have come as light into the world, so that everyone who believes in me should not remain in the darkness. I do not judge anyone who hears my words and does not keep them, for I came not to judge the world, but to save the world. The one who rejects me and does not receive my word has a judge; on the last day the word that I have spoken will serve as judge . . . (John 12:46-48, NRSV)

This is an interesting passage because here Jesus specifically addresses the question of those who reject him and "do not keep" his words. Jesus says that they have a judge, but that he is not that judge. How much less could his followers assume that authority.

Similarly, in the synoptic Gospels, Jesus condemns only those who would bring condemnation to others:

"But woe to you, scribes and Pharisees, hypocrites! For you lock people out of the kingdom of heaven. For you do not go in yourselves, and when others are going in, you stop them." (Matthew 23:13, NRSV)

"Woe to you lawyers! For you have taken away the key of knowledge; you did not enter yourselves, and you hindered those who were entering." (Luke 11:52, NRSV)

This is consistent with the nature of Christ's appearance as the mediator of the new covenant with its decree of the forgiveness of sins. After all, Jesus is the one who conditioned the disciples' forgiveness by God on their willingness to forgive others:

For if you forgive others their trespasses, your heavenly Father will also forgive you; but if you do not forgive others, neither will your Father forgive your trespasses. (Matthew 6:14-15, NRSV)

[2] In Charlesworth, *The Old Testament Pseudepigrapha*, Vol. 2, 119.

[3] It is clear that whatever Jesus may have meant by "blasphemy against the Holy Spirit" he was not referring to saying certain words (no matter how vile). He has just finished saying that whatever blasphemy people utter will be forgiven. In the parallel passage, Matthew 12:32 (NRSV), Jesus says, "Whoever speaks a word against the Son of Man will be forgiven," so he could not have meant bad doctrine or failure to acknowledge Jesus as Lord or Savior, either.

# BAPTISM INTO NEW LIFE

*T*o join a church and believe certain doctrines about
Christ is not sufficient to salvation. The community
of salvation is an invisible and spiritual fellowship
that overlaps with, but is not constrained by, the human societies that make up the visible church. We have already heard
Paul's teaching on the mysterious process through which human beings must pass in order to enter into this fellowship of
salvation:

> Do you not know that all of us who have been bap-
> tized into Christ Jesus were baptized into his death?
> Therefore we have been buried with him by baptism
> into death, so that, just as Christ was raised from the
> dead by the glory of the Father, so we too might walk
> in newness of life. (Romans 6:3-4, NRSV)

We have already heard how Jesus yielded to God's will by
offering the essential prayer "not my will but yours be done"
(Luke 22:42, NRSV; Mark 14:36; Matthew 26:39). In the
community of salvation, this yieldedness to God's will is not a
one-time event, but a daily way of life based on the model of
Jesus:

"I can do nothing on my own. As I hear, I judge; and my judgment is just, because I seek to do not my own will but the will of him who sent me." (John 5:30, NRSV)

This is the way of humility that Zephaniah offered as our hope for the Day of Judgment:

"Seek the Lord, all you humble of the land,
  who do his commands;
seek righteousness, seek humility;
  perhaps you may be hidden
  on the day of the Lord's wrath."
      (Zephaniah 2:3, NRSV; cf., 2 Samuel 22:28)

Humility is the key to salvation: it opens the door to righteousness and faith. Jesus not only shows us the way, but offers to be our companion on the journey:

Take my yoke upon you, and learn from me; for I am gentle and humble in heart, and you will find rest for your souls. (Matthew 11:29, NRSV).

There is another level of humility in the story of the cross, for it was not only as the human Son of Man that Jesus accepted God's will for him to die on the cross. If so, God would have punished an innocent man for other's guilt. Not so. According to the Gospel, Jesus was not only the human Messiah, he was also the form God took when God chose to appear among us in the flesh (John 1:1-3, 14; John 10:30; Titus 2:13; Hebrews 1:3; Revelation 22:13). This is the doctrine of the incarnation and it is, of course, an offense against any doctrine of God as omnipotent and unchangeable.[1] As God in human form, Jesus relinquished all the pride of place that was rightfully his, emptied himself of the rights of divinity and suffered even to the point of death (Philippians 2:6-8). Here, in its full glory, is the essentially incomprehensible claim of Christianity:

> For in him all the fullness of God was pleased to dwell, and through him God was pleased to reconcile to himself all things, whether on earth or in heaven, by making peace through the blood of his cross. (Colossians 1:19-20, NRSV)

In the person of Jesus of Nazareth, we see God choosing humility rather than power as the divinely sanctioned means by which the possibility of "goodness" comes into the world. Paul put it succinctly: "God was in Christ reconciling the world to Himself" (2 Corinthians 5:19, NAS).[2]

Jesus' death on the cross inaugurated the new covenant by which we are saved. But Jesus' followers must also take up their cross daily:

> Then he said to *them all,* "If any want to become my followers, let them deny themselves and take up their cross daily and follow me. For those who want to save their life will lose it, and those who lose their life for my sake will save it." (Luke 9:23-24, NRSV, my emphasis)

We bear the cross daily in the same way that Jesus did, by preferring God's will to our own. This is the way of humility. This is the way into the Kingdom of God. This is the essential baptism that we have to undergo if we wish to be saved. This is Paul's "baptism into death." This is what other biblical writers called, "the baptism of fire."

### Baptism in Fire

When God cast Adam and Eve out of Paradise, God barred the way to the tree of life:

> He drove out the man; and at the east of the garden of Eden he placed the cherubim, and a sword flaming and turning to guard the way to the tree of life. (Genesis 3:24, NRSV)

Likewise, before John saw the New Jerusalem with the tree of life in its midst, he saw a "lake of fire that burns with sulfur" (Revelation 19:20ff, NRSV). The way to the tree of life is through fire.

So, when God inaugurated the new covenant, the appropriate metaphor was fire. The prophet Malachi describes the coming of the messenger of the covenant this way:

> The messenger of the covenant in whom you delight—indeed, he is coming, says the Lord of hosts. But who can endure the day of his coming, and who can stand when he appears? For he is like a refiner's fire and like fullers' soap; he will sit as a refiner and purifier of silver, and he will purify the descendants of Levi and refine them like gold and silver, until they present offerings to the Lord in righteousness. (Malachi 3:2-3, NRSV)

The deep, inward, cleansing of heart and mind that Christian baptism symbolizes is this refiner's fire.

This is why the New Testament makes a distinction between the baptism of repentance introduced by John the Baptist and symbolized by water, and the baptism of the spirit introduced by Jesus and symbolized by fire. In announcing the coming of Jesus, John the Baptist said this:

> "I baptize you with water for repentance, but one
> who is more powerful than I is coming after me; I
> am not worthy to carry his sandals. He will baptize
> you with the Holy Spirit and fire. His winnowing
> fork is in his hand, and he will clear his threshing
> floor and will gather his wheat into the granary; but
> the chaff he will burn with unquenchable fire." (Mat-
> thew 3:11-12, NRSV; Luke 3:16-17)

Repentance is the response of a person who sees the moral chaos of his or her life as it appears in the light of the holiness of God. It is the act of one who says, "Left to my own devices, this is the mess I'm in! God help me!" But, of course, it is not the human cry for help that wipes the conscience clean or restores one's relationship with the Living God. That can only be done by the supernatural intervention of God. Repentance is the crucial human side of the equation—the act by which individuals invite God to implant the new heart within them. Repentance is necessary because it preserves human freedom in regard to salvation. But repentance, in itself, does not save.[3]

That is why John the Baptist himself pointed to another, different, and saving baptism. When he spoke of a baptism in fire, the Baptist had in mind the great days of purgation and judgment foretold in Zephaniah, Malachi, Amos, Daniel and 1 Enoch. In Jesus, however, that day of purgation became an inward event.

The Letter to the Hebrews talks about this same spiritual dynamic in yet another metaphor. It describes the living Word of God coming into the life of the believer as a two-edged sword:

> Indeed, the word of God is living and active, sharper
> than any two-edged sword, piercing until it divides
> soul from spirit, joints from marrow; it is able to

judge the thoughts and intentions of the heart. And
before him no creature is hidden, but all are naked
and laid bare to the eyes of the one to whom we must
render an account. (Hebrews 4:12-13, NRSV)

The living word of God is a light that exposes the evil fruit
of our false ideologies and imaginings and shows them to be
idolatrous. (See John 3:19-20.) It is sharp and piercing because it divides the individual's willfulness from God's will. It
is a refiner's fire. It burns up all that is false as chaff is burnt. It
is an inward and spiritual death of the will that is in rebellion
against God.

The way in which the baptism of fire actually works out in
an individual's life is demonstrated in the story of Abraham—
the man who, Paul tells us, was declared righteous by his faith
(Romans 4:22). It is an amazing story. Abraham stands at the
beginning of the history of salvation as the recipient of the
promise, "In you all the families of the earth shall be blessed"
(Genesis 12:3b, NRSV). In obedient response, Abraham and
Sarah left their homeland and went on a long journey to found
the family that this promise implied. Nothing worked out the
way they might have expected or imagined.

Already old when they left their home in Ur, Sarah and
Abraham endured thirty years of childlessness. Sarah de-
spaired in her barrenness and, following the custom of the
time, gave Abraham her slave woman Hagar to bear a child on
her behalf. Hagar duly gave birth to a son whom they named
Ishmael (Genesis 16). When Ishmael was fourteen years old,
Abraham and Ishmael were circumcised together in a celebration of God's covenant promise (Genesis 17:24-25). That very
year, Abraham and Sarah had their own child, Isaac. Sarah, of
course, was proud of her natural child and jealous of his rights.

She demanded that Abraham send Hagar and Ishmael away. This became an occasion of testing for Abraham.

Abraham did not approve of Sarah's plan, for he loved Ishmael and had come to see in Ishmael the fulfillment of God's promise. But God intervened to challenge Abraham's natural preference. The scripture relates:

> The matter was exceedingly bad in Avraham's eyes
> because of his son.
> But God said to Avraham:
> Do not let it be bad in your eyes concerning the lad
> and concerning your slave-woman;
> in all that Sara says to you, hearken to her voice;
> for it is through Yitzhak that seed will be called by
> your (name).
> (Genesis 21:11-12, Everett Fox)[4]

Still fearful that Hagar and his beloved Ishmael would perish, but acknowledging that what was "bad" in his own wisdom was "good" in the wisdom of God, Abraham, sent them out into the wilderness. Abraham did this on faith only, not knowing that God would intervene to protect Hagar and Ishmael from death. But that is what God did, for the scripture reports that "God was with the boy, and he grew up. . ." (Genesis 21:20, NRSV). God exceeded even this, for an angel announced God's will that Ishmael, too, would become a great nation. What was "bad" according to the natural wisdom of Abraham, God turned to "good."

A greater test was to follow, when God required Abraham to sacrifice Isaac.[5] The story is terrible and difficult:

> After these things God tested Abraham. He said to
> him, "Abraham!" And he said, "Here I am."

> He said, "Take your son, your only son Isaac, whom
> you love, and go to the land of Moriah, and offer him
> there as a burnt offering on one of the mountains
> that I shall show you." (Genesis 22:1-2, NRSV)

There is no softening this text; God requires Abraham to kill his son as a burnt offering.

The test cut deep: it required Abraham to forgo his—and society's—judgment of what is good (the love of parent for child) and, more radically yet, to abandon God's own covenant promise of descendents through which the nations would be blessed. On that promise, Abraham had uprooted his family, left the land of Haran, and spent his old age wandering in search of the promise. He had already forsaken his beloved child Ishmael; now Isaac was indeed his "only son." And, as the text says, Abraham loved Isaac.

Sacrifice is sacrificial to the extent that that which is sacrificed is loved or treasured by the one offering it up. Often God required the sacrifice of a particular blessing. When God commissioned Noah to save animals of every sort from the flood, God required Noah to sacrifice some of the very animals he had saved. God promised the Hebrew people a land flowing with milk and honey, and then God required them to offer up the best fruit of that land as a burnt offering. In biblical faith, the purpose of sacrifice is not to appease or reward God. Rather, by destroying as "holy unto the Lord" whatever is the end or purpose of our endeavors, hopes and love—even though the gift is from God—the faithful person is forcibly reminded that the gift must never take the place of the Holy One in our hearts. So, God required Abraham to sacrifice the very one who was the essence of the promise God had made to Abraham. Was Abraham's loyalty to God, or to the blessings promised by God?

Thus, "God tested Abraham." (Genesis 22:1, NRSV)
Abraham prepared to sacrifice Isaac. The only hint we have of the hope which sustained him, beyond reason or sight, is his answer to Isaac's question:

> "Where is the lamb for a burnt offering?"
>
> Abraham said, "God himself will provide the lamb for a burnt offering, my son." (Genesis 22:7b-8, NRSV)

It is not, however, clear that Abraham expects God to provide any other lamb than his own son. It is only after he had bound Isaac, and even raised the knife to kill him, that Abraham saw the ram that God provided as a substitutionary sacrifice.

The voice Abraham heard commanding him to sacrifice Isaac, now said, "Do not lay your hand on the lad or do anything to him; for now I know that you fear God ..." (Genesis 22:12, NRSV). Later, a messenger from God came to Abraham to confirm the promise that Abraham had proven himself willing to forsake. The messenger made the reason for God's blessing clear:

> "and by your offspring shall all the nations of the earth gain blessing for themselves, *because you have obeyed my voice*." (Genesis 22:18, NRSV, my emphasis)

Later, God appeared to the adult Isaac to reconfirm the promise and to remind us again of the basis for the blessing:

> and all the nations of the earth shall gain blessing for themselves through your offspring, *because Abraham obeyed my voice* [my emphasis] and kept my charge, my commandments, my statutes, and my laws." (Genesis 26:4b-5, NRSV, my emphasis)

The "voice" is the same *qol Yahweh* that Adam and Eve heard walking in the garden at the cool of day in Genesis 3:18. Yielding in obedience to that voice of God is the baptism of fire through which all must pass who would be saved.

Abraham is the spiritual father of those who live by faith because he was willing to abandon what he, personally, thought to be "good" in favor of obedience to the voice of God. Thus, Abraham's faith was "reckoned to him as righteousness, and he was called the friend of God" (James 2:21-24, NRSV). This is what it means for the righteous to live by faith (Romans 1:17).

Walking by faith requires us to forsake idolatry—which is the service of gods, ideologies, even ethics of our own creation—in radical abandonment to the voice of the living God. Isaiah encourages us:

> Seek the Lord while he may be found, call upon him while he is near; let the wicked forsake their way, and the unrighteous their thoughts; let them return to the Lord, that he may have mercy on them, and to our God, for he will abundantly pardon.
>
> For my thoughts are not your thoughts, nor are your ways my ways, says the Lord. For as the heavens are higher than the earth, so are my ways higher than your ways and my thoughts than your thoughts. (Isaiah 55:6-9, NRSV)

Abraham's story forces us to admit it: God's thoughts *are not* our thoughts. Of course, God does not put most people to so radical a test as Abraham faced on Mount Moriah. Nevertheless, the shift from relying upon our human wisdom and judgment to reliance upon the living word of God is a baptism in fire for all.

Jesus encourages his disciples to be aware of the cost and think it through:

> For which of you, desiring to build a tower, does not first sit down and count the cost, whether he has enough to complete it? (Luke 14:28, RSV)

The cost is the baptism in fire. It is the decision to move beyond calculating reason to faith, beyond the human knowledge of good and evil to a different kind of knowing—a knowing based on intimate acquaintance with the voice of the Good Shepherd.

Abraham's story shows that this baptism of fire, this baptism into death, is not a one-time event in the life of faith. From his first call to leave the land of Ur, through his dealings with Hagar and Ishmael, through his encounters with the angelic visitors who sojourned with him before rescuing Lot from Sodom, and so on up to the testing on Mount Moriah, Abraham had, again and again, to forsake his own wisdom and to trust the voice of the living God. Each of these encounters was a renewal of his baptism, a death to his own will. In each of these encounters, Abraham's intimate acquaintance with the voice of God grew.

Without that growth in intimacy with God, Abraham would not have been able to trust and follow the *qol Yahweh* when the words that were spoken were so very foreign as to demand the sacrifice of Isaac in fire. It is Molech—not Yahweh—who demands the sacrifice of children "passed through fire." (2 Kings 16:3; 23:10, NRSV).[6] Faith may require us to move beyond reason, but it does not lead us into the abyss of madness. Abraham did not know *how* God would prove to be faithful to the covenant at this time, but, by long acquaintance, Abraham knew that the voice he was hearing was the voice of

God and not of Molech. Blind faith would not have seen the substitutionary ram; rigid, doctrinal faith would not have had ears that remained open to hear the words, "Do not lay your hand upon the lad."

Faith does not require one to believe and obey *every* voice. God speaks to us as he did to Peter, James, and John at the Mount of Transfiguration, saying:

> "This is my Son, the Beloved;
>   listen *to him!*"
> (Mark 9:7, NRSV; see also Matthew 17:5; Luke
> 9:35, my emphasis.)

Faith requires us to "know the voice of the Good Shepherd" and to distinguish the *qol Yahweh* from any other. The ability to discern the voice of the Beloved from all others is learned over time, in the company of those who likewise are learning to walk in faith. It is learned by acquaintance with the word of God in scripture and by acquaintance with the word of God within the heart.

This intimacy with the living God is "the pearl of great price" that the wise merchant will "sell all" to obtain (Matthew 13:46, KJV). It is achieved by carrying the cross daily. It is the way into newness of life and ultimately to the restoration of all things. It is the way of salvation.

> Take care, brothers and sisters, that none of you may have an evil, unbelieving heart that turns away from the living God. But exhort one another every day, as long as it is called "today," so that none of you may be hardened by the deceitfulness of sin. For we have become partners of Christ, if only we hold our first confidence firm to the end. As it is said, "Today, if you hear his voice, do not harden your hearts as in the rebellion." (Hebrews 3:12-15, NRSV)

### The Gift of New Life

The majority of people experience life as a struggle against scarcity, and the world as a place of fear where violence may at any time be done to them; a world, therefore, where it is the course of wisdom to hoard what goods we can and to organize ourselves into bands armed for self-protection. Constant struggle and fear results in anxiety: a sense of the deficit of love. But since love is a more fundamental need for human survival than even food, people may seek love in many destructive and ultimately violent ways.

All of this is the fruit of sin. In the end, sin does not consist in the myriad of specific destructive actions. Sin is always, fundamentally, idolatry: turning to other gods (including ourselves) for what properly comes from God alone—love, security, and the wisdom to decide what is good and what is evil. That is original sin, and it always results in death.

In contrast, God's intention in creation was to make a place for loving fellowship between himself and a community of people. In that fellowship, we walk together enjoying abundance, expressing creativity and love. Because the essential condition of genuine love is freedom, that too is part of God's intention from the beginning. Inevitably, freedom includes the possibility of choosing against God himself, so God continues to extend even that freedom until the end of history. The freedom to sin is the penultimate sign of God's love.

The ultimate sign of God's love is the cross. In Jesus Christ, God decisively entered human history to inaugurate a renewed relationship—a new covenant—with humankind. The bases of this new relationship are three actions which God took on his own initiative and by his own power. These are: 1) to replace the inner seat of the individual human will that has been hardened by fear with hearts of flesh capable of hearing and obeying God's voice; 2) to be continuously present in each person's life through the pouring out of the Holy Spirit so that the believer can have direct access to God's leadings; and, having thus uprooted original sin, 3) to remove the guilt and bitterness attached to our many sinful acts, by the word of forgiveness. Freed from the prisons of fear, hate, and anxiety that sin has created, people can start again to live the life God intended for us all from the beginning of creation.

The only way to evade this new covenant (the only "unforgivable sin") is to utterly reject the loving presence of God. This God also allows out of the tragic necessity of love. But when, in the ever-renewed freedom of forgiveness, human beings turn again toward God and accept the gifts of a new heart and of God's presence as their inward teacher, they come to experience salvation in its many forms. This is eternal life.

Communion with God restored, people become new creations in Christ. In the community of their fellow believers, they come to experience—at least in part—the abundance and peace that is pictured for us in the story of the garden of Eden, where the *qol Yahweh* walks with humankind at the time of the moving of the spirit.

We face constant decisions and choices, minute by minute, day by day. As free agents in a complex world, it is inevitable that in the past we will have made decisions contrary to the will of God and that in the future we will do so again. Even though we know the love and the heart of God, and even though it is our desire to live rightly before God, because we have been bruised by the consequences of sin and because our healing is always only partial until the final day is accomplished, we will from time to time choose to go our own way. God knows this.

It is therefore always true that we are sinners saved by grace. The capstone of the new covenant is not the promise that God will write the law in our hearts, for we will often evade it even so. Nor is it the promise that God will always be present with us, for as much when we sin as when we do well, we are still in the presence of God. Rather, the capstone of the covenant is the word of forgiveness that tells us that God will never let go of us, that the new covenant is in fact eternal and cannot be broken. There is nothing that we can do to separate ourselves from the love of God.

> If God is for us, who is against us? He who did not withhold his own Son, but gave him up for all of us, will he not with him also give us everything else? . . .

> For I am convinced that neither death, nor life, nor angels, nor rulers, nor things present, nor things to come, nor powers, nor height, nor depth, nor anything else in all creation, will be able to separate us from the love of God in Christ Jesus our Lord. (Romans 8:31-32, 38, NRSV)

The atonement between God and humanity that God accomplished in Jesus on the cross brings to fulfillment the new covenant promise. Through this sacrifice, God speaks directly to the hard and alienated heart of all humankind, saying definitively what God has always said, "I will be your God, and you will be my people."

When God has taken all judgment upon himself, there is nothing left to fear, there is no more cause for hardness of heart. Through his sacrifice on the cross, God takes hearts of stone and turns them to hearts of flesh.

God says, "You will all know me from the least to the greatest" (Jeremiah 31:34, NRSV). Because of the sacrifice on the cross, we know that not as a threat, but as a cry of recognition and of love. Because Jesus died and rose again, God pours out the Holy Spirit in unlimited measure without distinction of class, race, gender, ritual, or even creed. God cries out to all: "I will be your God; learn of me."

No righteousness of our own, no deeds of love, no right doctrine, no abasement of self, no exultation in worship, can earn us the love of God; before any of that, God has already chosen to love us. That was a choice God made even before the creation of the world. There is nothing to earn. The decision has been made: "I will be your God."

Beyond all the choices that we make and all the freedom that is ours, beyond the possibility and even the inevitability that we will sin and will be sinned against, there is a reality that it is impossible for a human being to evade: we live by the mercy and the forgiveness of God. "God is love" (1 John 4:8-16, NRSV).

In this world, the greatest gift that we can receive is to live in the context of a community that (like God) knows the truth of who we are, and that *even so* (like God) shows us mercy, grace and forgiveness. The community of genuine love must acknowledge the reality and the evil of sin in general, and, to some extent, our sins in particular. Only then can the community combine grace with truth, and reveal itself as the community of God's chosen. When those who know us in truth still offer us mercy, we have met God.

When we have met God, we have met the law of God. It is not possible that God should be only grace and not truth, any more than it is possible that the God who became flesh for our sakes and willingly suffered death on the cross, should be only truth and not grace.

Having come into the community of both grace and truth we are enfolded into a life that begins to reflect the intentions of God from the beginning of creation. We begin to find our hearts opening up in ways that our alienated and suspicious psyches could never have imagined. We feel the various compulsions that had so tightly bound us as we desperately grasped after love gradually losing their grip upon our lives. Experiencing love offered without condition (which means being loved by those who know us in truth for the sinners we are, so there is no more pretense), we discover that we can enjoy, and perhaps even love, other people for themselves and not simply as ends to meet our cravings. Sexual misconduct drops away. Loneliness is overwhelmed by friendship.

Enfolded in the community of grace, we discover that the fearful grasping after possessions is no longer necessary or satisfying, and we begin to exhibit a new simplicity of life and generosity that surprises both ourselves and our former companions. Relieved of fear because of the new experience of the abundance and generosity we are discovering in the community of faith, we let down the barriers of hatred and enmity that we have drawn up between ourselves and the outer world. We become agents of reconciliation, and, thus, to know ourselves as the children of God.

And when we stumble, we are not surprised or horrified. We already know the truth: we are sinners, alive solely because of the mercy of the One who is love. We know ourselves as forgiven, and we forgive ourselves. We are back to the beginning.

We have been born again.

¹ Islam, for instance, is appalled at this doctrine. Whereas, Islam holds Jesus Christ in high esteem as a prophet, the Qur'an insists that he was taken to Allah before he died, so that he only appeared to have been crucified (Surah 4:157-8). This is to safeguard the doctrine that Allah could not have suffered, which is the main point of Surah 5:17.

In blasphemy indeed are those that say that Allah is Christ the son of Mary. Say: "Who then hath the least power against Allah, if His will were to destroy Christ the son of Mary, his mother, and all everyone that is on the earth? For to Allah belongeth the dominion of the heavens and the earth, and all that is between. He createth what He pleaseth. For Allah hath power over all things."

Surah 19:35 makes clear the offense of the Christian doctrine that Christ is the Son of God: "It is not befitting to (the majesty of) Allah that He should beget a son" (The hypertexted version of *The Meanings Of The Holy Qur'an* by Abdullah Yusufali at http://www.islamicity.com/mosque/quran/).

² In Greek, the preposition *en* can mean either "in" (locative) or "by means of" (instrumental) and RSV and NRSV both give "in Christ God was reconciling the world to himself"—understanding the phrase "in Christ" in the instrumental sense rather than in the locative sense of our translation. However, in v. 18, Paul has already said "God, who reconciled us to himself *through/dia* Christ" where the preposition clearly bears the instrumental sense. In verse 19, I think that the KJV ASV, NAS, NJB translators correctly understood that Paul is now expanding and correcting the earlier verse, and intending to say: that is, God was *in* Christ.

³ Paul says repentance leads into salvation/*eiv sotherian* (2 Corinthianss 7:10).

⁴ Everett Fox, *The Five Books of Moses, The Schocken Bible: Vol. I*, (Schocken Books: New York), 1995. Fox's translation, always sensitive to underlying Hebrew terms, shows the relationship between the verb, be bad/*yawrah*,, and its parent noun, evil/*rah*, which appears notably in "the tree of the knowledge of good and evil" (Genesis 2:9, NAS).

[5] A particularly helpful commentary on this incident is Soren Kierkegaard, *Fear and Trembling,* translated by Alastair Hannay, Penguin Books, New York, 1985.

[6] Indeed, presumably to protect the goodness of God, the Book of Jubilees 17:15-18:12 (second century B.C.) puts responsibility on "Prince Mastema" (i.e., Satan) for suggesting that Abraham should be tested in this way.

# Appendix 1:
# Discussion Questions

### Introduction

1. What personal experience of God or Spirit has spoken to you of God's present reality in the world?

2. Do you experience God mostly as grace and love? Do you experience God mostly as truth, justice, or righteousness? What experiences have brought you to this understanding?

### Chapter 1: Two Gardens and Two Trees

1. Pick one of the qualities of life in the Garden "before the fall" that feels important to you today. How would you like to see it grow in your own life?

2. How do you understand the term "original sin"? Have you experienced it?

3. What do you think is the role of the serpent in the story of the Garden of Eden? Does the serpent act this way in our lives, today?

### Chapter 2: Salvation in this World and the Next

1. In scripture, "covenant" refers to the relationship between God and a group of people. What does it mean for God to declare that a covenant has been "broken"? Do you think that this has implications for us today?

2. What does the phrase, "the day of the Lord" mean? Have you, personally, ever experienced a time of "visitation" from God?

3. The Sadducees and the Pharisees disagreed about whether or not there will be a bodily resurrection. What do you believe happens at death and thereafter? How important is this to you?

## Chapter 3: *The New Covenant*

1. Are you optimistic about the human capacity to do good, or do you share Jeremiah's pessimism about the "perversity" of the human will?

2. As you meditate on Jesus' death on the cross, what response do you find welling up within you? What meaning does it have for you personally?

3. How have you experienced Jesus' words of blessing or forgiveness in your life?

4. Have you felt the inward presence of the "Counselor"? What of "tongues" or "prophecy"? If not, have you observed them in others? What was your reaction?

5. Discuss the statement that the "linchpin of salvation" is "attending to the living word of God." What does this mean? Is right belief essential, or are there other things more fundamental to salvation?

## Chapter 4: *The Sign of the Listening Community*

1. In what ways has Jesus brought you into community? Has your observation of the way people of faith live their lives affected your willingness to believe in Jesus' salvation?

2. To what extent does the fellowship of your church reflect Paul's insight that, through the blood of Jesus, those who were socially and religiously different from each other have been brought together as equals?

3. How have you experienced mutual submission?

4. Do you make room for the possibility that anyone may speak the word of God? How do you "weigh" the truth (or prophetic authority) of what is said?

## Chapter 5: The Sign of the Bountiful Community

1. How do you make a place for "Sabbath" rest in your life? Have you experienced God's miraculous provision for your material needs?

2. Discuss how you could implement tithing as a joyful party, as described in Deuteronomy 14. How would you include the poor?

3. How did Jesus implement the Jubilee among his followers and in the people he recruited? How could we do the same?

4. The angel in Revelation calls for the faithful to "come out" of Mystery Babylon. Name some of the economic injustices you see around you. How could you support one another in "coming out" from them and a lifestyle based in materialism?

## Chapter 6: The Sign of the Peaceable Community

1. Elisha prayed that God would "open the eyes" of his servant to see God's angelic hosts. Have you had personal experiences, or seen events, that have opened your eyes to God's power to save people from enemies (or physical danger) in big or small ways?

2. Since the 4th century, most of the Church has accepted a theory of "just war" which states that it is permissible for Christians to go to war in some circumstances. In light of this chapter, do you believe that to be biblical and to reflect Jesus' will for the Church?

3. Compare the political situation King Ahaz faced when Isaiah offered him the sign of Immanuel with the real threats

of enemies (terrorists and others) we face today. How should the church assist the nation when the nation faces difficult questions of war and peace?

4. Paul says, "the weapons we fight with are not of this world." What are the weapons Christ gives us to fight with? What is the goal of the fight?

## Chapter 7: *The Sign of the Community of Grace and Truth*

1. Many people have been hurt by judgmental attitudes of church members. Others have felt morally abandoned when the church fails to be clear about right and wrong. Have you ever received or offered discipline of the sort described in Matthew 18? Was it helpful or hurtful? Why?

2. How is Jesus' miraculous authority to "bind and loose" expressed in the context of your faith community? Or, if you feel it is lacking, what first steps might you take to recover it?

3. What are some "false communities" you are involved in? What does Jesus say defines the true community of faith?

4. Jesus welcomed the most vulnerable and wounded into his circle; the pharisaic church requires people to pretend they are perfect. Where does your church fit on this continuum? Where, in your experience, do you feel safe confessing sin?

## Chapter 8: *Baptism into New Life*

1. Has God shown you that something you thought was "good" was, in fact, "evil"—or the other way around? How did you learn this?

2. Have you ever had to pray, "Your will be done" even though you had a strong preference for a specific outcome? What happened?

3. What does it mean to be "born again"?

# Appendix 2:
# Questions Concerning
# the Saved Life

*T*he Friends (or Quaker) movement is fiercely non-creedal and would be even less inclined to subscribe to a particular theory of atonement than the Christian church in general. However, for my part, I will happily claim the influence of Friends in the development of my understanding of the saving work of Christ.

In line with the new covenant insistence that God speaks directly to each believer, Friends have developed a practice of posing to themselves a series of questions (traditionally termed, "queries") for self-examination. This is not conceived of as an individual spiritual exercise but rather as a means whereby the community seeks truth together, and out of which emerges a style of living that Friends call "testimonies" to Christ's work in their lives.

Friends often begin their meetings for church business by reading one or more of these questions and then waiting in a period of expectant and reflective silence. This is not a time for discussion. Rather, the group is listening together for the living Word. As the Holy Spirit prompts, sometimes individuals will speak to how God has been moving in their lives in relationship to the issue posed. Such speaking is most helpful when it is simple and personal. When the others allow some period of quiet after each contribution, that allows room for the Holy Spirit to bring conviction to the hearts of those present.

The following questions are culled from several Friends' books of "Faith and Practice."[1] As such, they have gone through a careful process of approval by the regional groupings of Friends meetings that are responsible for church discipline. In hopes that they will serve to extend fruitful consideration of the matters raised in this book, I commend them to you, and also the practice of considering them with others in a context of worshipful sharing.

### God's Saving Presence

Do you strive for the constant realization of God's presence in your life? Are you obedient to the leading and sensitive to the timing of the Holy Spirit? (IYM)

Do you make a place in your daily life for reading, meditation, and waiting upon God in prayer, that you may know more of the presence and guidance of the Holy Spirit? (LYM)

Are our homes places where the presence of God is felt by those who live there and those who visit there? (NYYM)

Do you come to meeting[s for worship] with heart and mind prepared for communion with God and fellowship with one another? (IYM)

### The Inclusive Community

As Christians do you consistently practice principles of love and good will toward all . . . ? (IYM)

Do you try to make the stranger feel at home among you? (LYM)

Does your attitude toward people of other races and gender indicate your belief in their right to equal opportunity? (IYM)

Do we do all in our power to secure civil rights for all?
(NYYM)

Are you patient and considerate, even towards those whom
you find it hard to like and those who seem to you unloving
and ungrateful? (LYM)

### Discipline and Mutual Submission

As followers of Jesus Christ do you love and respect one
another? (IYM)

Do you . . . live in a way that promotes the sanctity and
health of marriage and family life? (IYM)

Do you discipline your mind and body to serve as instruments of the Lord? Do you avoid pornography? (NWYM)

Do you who are married yield to each other in decisions
and build up each other as individuals, always cherishing your
common bond? (NWYM)

Are love and unity fostered among us? If differences arise,
do we endeavor to reconcile them in a spirit of love and truth?
(NYYM)

Do we avoid talebearing, and are we careful of the reputa-
tion of others? (NYYM)

Are your meetings for business conducted in a spirit of
worship and a united search for God's leading in transacting
the affairs of the meeting? (IYM)

### Sabbath Rest

Do we partake of the joy of the love of God and make our
lives a celebration of the sharing of this love? (NYYM)

How do you actively avoid self-destructive stresses in your
life? (IYM)

Do you avoid such undue expansion of your business and social responsibilities as to endanger your personal integrity or detract from your Christian commitment? (IYM)

### Honoring God's Provision

Is your life marked by simplicity? Are you free from the burden of unnecessary possessions? (NWYM)

Do you use care in the materials you consume and the materials you discard to maintain the integrity of God's creation? (IYM)

Do you refuse to let the prevailing culture and media dictate your needs and values? (NWYM)

Do we make ourselves available in a tender and caring way when we sense a need for assistance in time of trouble? Do we trust each other enough to make our needs known to someone in our meeting? (NYYM)

### Jubilee

Do you regard your possessions as given to you in trust and do you part with them freely for the needs of others? (LYM)

Are you sensitive to the material needs of those within the meeting and in the local community? (IYM)

Are you personally scrupulous and responsible in the use of money entrusted to you, and are you careful not to defraud the public revenue? (LYM)

Are you concerned that economic systems function to sustain and enrich all life? (IYM)

### Peace

Do we foster reverence for life? (NYYM)

Do you observe and teach the Friends testimony against military training and service, making clear that war is incompatible with the spirit and teachings of the Gospel? (NWYM)

Are we exerting our influence in favor of settlement of all differences by truly nonviolent methods? (NYYM)

Do you live in the virtue of that life and power that takes away the occasion of all wars? (LYM)

---

[1] Friends highest authority is vested in regional associations of churches called Yearly Meetings. They publish books of "faith and practice" or "discipline" which lay out the procedures of church government and also describe the faith held by that group of Friends. The source of each of the questions quoted below is given in parentheses and is keyed to the books listed in Sources, page 246.

# Sources

### General

Brown, Colin, gen. ed. *The New international Dictionary of New Testament Theology.* 3 volumes. Grand Rapids, MI: Zondervan Publishing House, 1976.

Bushell, Michael S. and Michael D. Tan, programmers. *Bible Works™ for Windows™* Copyright ©1992-1999 *Bible Works,* L.L.c.

Charlesworth, James, ed., *The Old Testament Pseudepigrapha.* 2 volumes, Garden City, NY: Doubleday Company, Inc., 1985.

Nestle, Eberhard, et. al. *Apparatus of the Nestle-Aland Novum Testamentum Graece,* 26 edition, Stuttgart, Germany: Deutshe Bibelstiftung, 1979.

Sproul, R.C., ed. *Getting the Gospel Right: The Tie That Binds Evangelicals Together.* See Appendix 2, "The Gospel of Jesus Christ: An Evangelical Celebration." Grand Rapids, MI: Baker Books, 1999.

"The Teaching of the Twelve Apostles, Commonly Called the Didache" in Cyril C. Richardson, ed. and trans., *Early Christian Fathers,* New York: Macmillan Publishing Co., 1970.

Yusufali, Abdullah. *The Meanings of The Holy Qur'an.* Hypertexted version at http://www.islamicity.com/ mosque/ quran/ accessed May 2000.

### Friends books of discipline

(IYM) *Faith and Practice of Indiana Yearly Meeting of the Religious Society of Friends,* Muncie, IN: Indiana Yearly Meeting of Friends, 1998.

(LYM) *Church government, London Yearly Meeting of the Religious Society of Friends,* London: London Yearly Meeting, 1967.

(NYYM) *Faith and Practice: The Book of Discipline of the New York Yearly Meeting of the Religious Society of Friends,* New York: New York Yearly Meeting, 1995.

(NWYM) *Faith and Practice: a Book of Christian Discipline, Northwest Yearly Meeting of Friends Church,* Newberg, OR: The Barclay Press, 1987.

# INDEX OF SCRIPTURE CITATIONS

**Genesis**

| | |
|---|---|
| 1:1-4 | 24 |
| 1:2 | 17 |
| 1-2:4 | 16 |
| 2:7 | 16 |
| 2:8 | 13 |
| 2:9 | 18, 24, 232 |
| 2:12 | 18 |
| 2:15 | 16 |
| 2:16-17 | 24 |
| 2:18 | 20 |
| 2:19 | 17 |
| 2:20 | 20 |
| 2:24 | 22 |
| 2:25 | 22 |
| 3:1-3 | 23 |
| 3:8 | 29 |
| 3:8-10 | 22 |
| 3:11-13 | 23 |
| 3:16 | 20, 64 |
| 3:17-19 | 17 |
| 3:18 | 224 |
| 3:22 | 26 |
| 3:24 | 31, 200, 218 |
| 4:3-8 | 30 |
| 4-11 | 26 |
| 4:23-24 | 18 |
| 6:4-5 | 19 |
| 6:6 | 19 |
| 6:11-13 | 19 |
| 12:1-3 | 36 |
| 12:3 | 93, 220 |
| 12:12-13 | 37 |
| 15:9-18 | 69 |
| 16 | 220 |
| 17:1-14 | 37 |
| 17:14 | 114 |
| 17:24-25 | 220 |
| 18:19 | 37 |
| 19:30ff | 37 |
| 21:11-12 | 221 |
| 21:20 | 221 |
| 22:1 | 223 |
| 22:1-2 | 221-222 |
| 22:7-8 | 223 |
| 22:12 | 223 |
| 22:18 | 223 |
| 26:4-5 | 223 |
| 27 | 37 |
| 41:48-49 | 129 |
| 44:5 | 37 |
| 49:5 | 34 |
| 49:25 | 20 |
| 50:20 | 129 |

**Exodus**

| | |
|---|---|
| 2:17 | 39 |
| 6:7 | 94 |
| 12:29 | 157 |
| 14:10 | 157 |
| 14:13-14 | 157 |
| 14:21-30 | 40 |
| 14:30 | 158 |
| 15:1-3 | 158 |
| 15:26 | 41 |
| 16:2-3 | 129-130 |
| 16:4 | 138 |
| 16:8 | 147 |
| 16:11-31 | 130 |
| 16:17-20 | 139 |
| 18:16 | 113 |
| 20:1-17 | 41 |
| 20:1-3 | 41 |
| 20:17 | 144 |
| 20:5 | 41 |
| 20:7 | 112 |
| 24:6-8 | 69 |

**Leviticus**

| | |
|---|---|
| 7:13 | 124 |
| 11:44-45 | 41 |
| 16 | 133 |
| 19:18 | 206 |
| 19:2-19 | 41 |
| 19:34 | 206 |
| 20:10 | 207 |
| 20:11 | 207 |
| 22:31-33 | 41 |
| 25:14-23 | 134 |
| 25:25-55 | 151 |

25:4. . . . . . . . . . . . .132
25:9-10. . . . . . . . .133
26:3-18. . . . . . . . . .41
26:12 . . . . . . . . . . .94
26:42ff . . . . . . . . . .94

Numbers
11:7. . . . . . . . . . . . .33
11:25 . . . . . . . . . . .106
11:27-29 . . . . . . . .106
13:33 . . . . . . . . . . .33
15:16 . . . . . . . . . . .206

Deuteronomy
5:1-10. . . . . . . . . . .41
5:5-7. . . . . . . . . . . .41
5:11. . . . . . . . . . . .112
5:15. . . . . . . . . . . .126
5:21. . . . . . . . . . . .144
6:1-5. . . . . . . . . . . .41
6:12-13. . . . . . . . .192
7:6-8. . . . . . . . . . . .93
13:1-5. . . . . . . . . .112
13:1ff . . . . . . . . . .120
14:25-26 . . . . . . . .127
14:28-29 . . . . . . . .127
15:1-11. . . . . .131-132
15:4. . . . . . . 134, 146
15:12-17 . . . 103, 151
15:15-19 . . . . . . . .89
18:20 . . . . . . . . . . .112
18:22 . . . . . . . . . . .120
19:16 . . . . . . . . . . .33
20 . . . . . . . . . . . . .190
20:2-8. . . . . . . . . .159
22:22 . . . . . . . . . .207

Joshua
5:13-15. . . . . . . . .163
13-19 . . . . . . . . . .133

Judges
2:16. . . . . . . . . . . .42

4 . . . . . . . . . . . . . .159
7:2. . . . . . . . . . . . .159
7:5-7. . . . . . . .159-160
8:10. . . . . . . . . . . .159

1 Samuel
8:5. . . . . . . . . . . . .160
8:7. . . . . . . . . . . . .107
8:11-17. . . . . .160-161
10:1-2. . . . . . . . . . .42
10:6-7. . . . . . . . .42-43
17:37 . . . . . . . . . . .161
17:45-47 . . . . . . . .161

2 Samuel
3:18. . . . . . . . . . . .43
7:8-13. . . . . . . . . . .43
7:14-15. . . . . . . . . .44
12:1-12. . . . . . . . . .44
22:28 . . . . . . . . . . .216
23:5. . . . . . . . . . . .44
24 . . . . . . . . . . . . .191

1 Kings
3:9. . . . . . . . . . . . .113
11:3. . . . . . . . . . . .45
11:5. . . . . . . . . . . .46
18 . . . . . . . . . . . . .140
22:6ff . . . . . . . . . .112

2 Kings
2:11. . . . . . . . . . . .62
6:15-17. . . . . . . . .163
6:18-23. . . . . .163-164
16:2-4. . . . . . . . . .167
16:3. . . . . . . . . . . .225
16:5-7. . . . . . . . . .165
16:7-9. . . . . . . . . .166
17:4. . . . . . . . . . . .191
23:10 . . . . . . 191, 225

2 Chronicles
9:13-27. . . . . . . . . .45

10:4. . . . . . . . . . . .46
10:23 . . . . . . . . . . .162
20:12 . . . . . . . . . . .162
20:15-17 . . . . . . . .162
32:1-22. . . . . . . . .164

Job
17:12ff . . . . . . . . . .62
26:6. . . . . . . . . . . .33

Psalms
2:7-9. . . . . . . . . . . .73
12:5. . . . . . . . . . . .131
19:7-11. . . . . . . . . .38
30:3. . . . . . . . . . . .92
33:16-17 . . . . . . . .156
44:4-7. . . . . . . . . .156
50:10-23 . . . .124-125
51:1-12. . . . . . .44-45
54:4. . . . . . . . . . . .20
82:3-4, 8. . . . . . . .173
103:2-3. . . . . . . . .203
104:24-28 . . . . . . .124
115:17 . . . . . . . . . .62
118:10-16 . . .176-177
118:25-26 . . . . . .176
132:9, 16 . . . . . . .196

Proverbs
3:13-20. . . . . . . . .34
5:18-19. . . . . . . . .21
11:31 . . . . . . . . . . .60

Song of Solomon
8:1-3. . . . . . . . . . . .21

Isaiah
2:1-4. . . . . . .179-180
3:14-15. . . . .134-135
5:8-14. . . . . . . . . .135
7:4. . . . . . . . . . . . .167
7:14. . . . . . . . . . . .166
7:15. . . . . . . . . . . .34

8:12-15......167-168
8:5-8............168
10:3.............50
10:22............60
13:6.............50
25:6-8..........125
26:19............62
28:7f...........120
30:10..........112
31:5-9..........165
40:1-3..........170
42:1-4...........52
44:7f...........120
45:22-23.........91
46:7.............34
51:3-4...........86
52:7-8..........179
52:13-15.........52
53:4-6...........52
55:1-3..........148
55:6-9..........224
59:15-18........184
61:1, 10........196
63:1-6..........185
64:6.............66
65:17-25......53-54

**Jeremiah**
1:9.............111
2:11-34.........191
4:10, 19-20......50
5:1-29.........48-49
5:31............112
6:14............165
7:3-15..........50
7:9-15..........177
7:11............177
7:16............178
7:23-24.........94
8:11............165
11:10........49-50
17:9-10..........65
19:5............191

20:9............111
23:21...........112
30:12-15........66
30:17, 22.......66
31:31-33........68
31:32...........95
31:33...........68
31:34.....60, 74, 81,
83, 105, 229
32:27..........154
32:39-42.......153
33:9...........136
34:12-17....135-136
34:18......136, 152
34:21..........136
46:10...........50

**Lamentations**
3:26-41, 64-65...174

**Ezekiel**
11:19-20......66-67
16:60-61.........94
22:6-15.........152
30:3............51
34:20-23.......137
36:25-28........67
36:26..........153
36:26-36.......136
36:35-36.......153
47:1-12.........34

**Daniel**
7:9-14........71-72
12:1-2..........62

**Hosea**
1:7............165
8:1.............48
13:9-11........191

**Joel**
2:1.............50

2:28-29.........105
3:9-16..........192

**Amos**
2:6-8............47
3:8.............111
4:1-3............48
5:14.............47
5:18-20..........51
5:21-24..........47
7:15............111
9:11-12.........115

**Micah**
3:5............120
4:1-4.......179-180

**Zephaniah**
1:14-17..........51
2:3............216
3:17-19......156-157

**Haggai**
2:21-22..........53

**Zechariah**
4:6............157
9:9-10..........175
9:11-16.....175-176
14:1-7..........53
14:21..........178

**Malachi**
3:2-3..........218
4:1.............50

**Matthew**
1:21-23........169
3:2.........86, 178
3:3...........170
3:11-12........219
4:8-10.........170
4:17.......86, 178

5:2-8 . . . . . . . . . . . . .73
5:5 . . . . . . . . . . . . . .190
5:9-12 . . . . . . . . . . .190
5:14 . . . . . . . . . . . . .97
5:22 . . . . . . . . . . . . .56
5:27-28 . . . . . . . . .207
5:39-41 . . . . . . . . .173
5:43-49 . . . . . . . . .181
6:9-10 . . . . . . . . . .172
6:9-13 . . . . . . . . . .138
6:14-15 . . . . . . . .214
6:19-24 . . . . . .139-140
6:22-23 . . . . . . . . .152
7:15 . . . . . . . . . . . .113
7:16f . . . . . . . . . . .120
8:5-13 . . . . . . . . . .181
9:5-6 . . . . . . . . . . .203
9:9-13 . . . . . . . . . .141
10 . . . . . . . . . . . . . .95
10:1-8 . . . . . . . . . . .88
10:7 . . . . . . . . .86, 178
10:15 . . . . . . . . . . . .56
10:16-31 . . . .171-172
10:24-25 . . . . . . . .188
10:34-37 . . . . . . . .209
10:38 . . . . . . . . . . .178
11:29 . . . . . . . . . . .216
12:24 . . . . . . . . . . .201
12:26-29 . . . . . . . .201
12:32 . . . . . . 119, 214
12:34-72 . . . . . . . . .56
13:41-43 . . . . . . . . .56
13:46 . . . . . . . . . . .226
14:13ff . . . . . . . . .145
16:16 . . . . . . . . . . .200
16:17-18 . . . . . . . .200
16:19 . . . . . . . . . . .201
16:23 . . . . . . . . . . .171
16:24 . . . . . . . . . . .178
17:5 . . . . . . . . . . . .226
18:1-5 . . . . . . . . . .107
18:8-9 . . . . . . . . . . .56
18:14ff . . . . . . . . .119

18:15 . . . . . . . . . . .198
18:16 . . . . . . . . . . .198
18:17 . . . . . . . . . . .198
18:18-20 . . . . . . . .199
18:21-22 . . . . . . . .209
19:21 . . . . . . . . . . .144
19:25-26 . . . . . . . .154
19:28 . . . . . . . . . . . .72
20:1-15 . . . . . . . . .152
20:20-28 . . . .107-108
21:1-17 . . . . . . . . .175
21:9 . . . . . . . . . . . .176
21:13 . . . . . . . . . . .177
22:2-10 . . . . .195-196
22:11-12 . . . . . . . .196
22:13 . . . . . . . . . . .197
22:23 . . . . . . . . . . . .55
22:32 . . . . . . . . . . . .55
22:36ff . . . . . . . . .206
23:13 . . . . . . . . . . .213
23:37 . . . . . . . . . . . .95
24:11 . . . . . . 113, 120
25:31-36 . . . . . . . .147
26:39 . . . . . . 189, 215
26:52-53 . . . . . . . .169
27:52 . . . . . . . . . . . .62
28:20 . . . . . . . . . . .111

**Mark**
1:2-3 . . . . . . . . . . . .170
1:15 . . . . . . . . .86, 179
2:28 . . . . . . . . . . . .119
2:9-11 . . . . . . . . . .203
3:21 . . . . . . . . . . . .208
3:28-29 . . . . . . . . .208
3:33-34 . . . . . . . . .209
5:25-34 . . . . . . . . . .87
6:31ff . . . . . . . . . .145
8:11ff . . . . . . . . . .145
8:33 . . . . . . . . . . . .171
8:34 . . . . . . . . . . . .178
9:7 . . . . . . . . . . . . .226
9:35-37 . . . . . . . . .107

10:17 . . . . . . . . . . .144
10:21 . . . . . . . . . . .144
10:42-45 . . . .107-108
10:26-27 . . . . . . . .154
11:1-18 . . . . . . . . .175
11:9 . . . . . . . . . . . .176
11:17 . . . . . . . . . . .177
12:18 . . . . . . . .55, 178
12:25 . . . . . . . . . . . .62
12:26-27 . . . . . . . . .55
13:22 . . . . . . . . . . .113
14:36 . . . . . . 189, 215

**Luke**
1:72 . . . . . . . . . . . . .94
2:13-14 . . . . . . . . .169
2:34 . . . . . . . . . . . .192
3:4-6 . . . . . . . . . . .170
3:16-17 . . . . . . . . .219
4:6-8 . . . . . . . . . . .170
4:18 . . . . . . . . . . . .196
4:22 . . . . . . . . . . . . .99
4:25-30 . . . . . .99-100
5:23-24 . . . . . . . . .203
6:15 . . . . . . . . . . . .193
6:27-35 . . . . . . . . .181
7:11-16 . . . . . . . . . .96
7:22 . . . . . . . . . . . .137
7:47-50 . . . . . . . . .210
8:1-3 . . . . . . . . . . .145
9:1 . . . . . . . . . . . . .202
9:1-5 . . . . . . . . . . . .95
9:10ff . . . . . . . . . .145
9:23 . . . . . . . . . . . .178
9:23-24 . . . . . . . . .217
9:35 . . . . . . . . . . . .226
9:46-48 . . . . . . . . .106
9:54-55 . . . . . .170-171
10:1-16 . . . . . . . . . .95
10:18 . . . . . . . . . . .202
10:1-9 . . . . . . . . . . .88
10:9 . . . . . 89, 179, 202
10:25-37 . . . . . . . .206

11:2-4 . . . . . . . . . .138
11:52 . . . . . . . . . . .213
12:10 . . . . . . . . . . .119
12:15-21 . . . . . . . .140
13:15-16 . . . . . . . .202
14:16-24 . . . . . . . .128
14:26 . . . . . . . . . . .209
14:28 . . . . . . . . . . .225
15:2. . . . . . . . . . . .119
16:1-9 . . . . . .143-144
17:11-19 . . . . . . . . .88
17:24-35 . . . . . . . . .56
18:13-14 . . . . . . . .211
18:22 . . . . . . . . . . .144
18:26-27 . . . . . . . .154
19:1-10. . . . . . . . . .142
19:29-46 . . . . . . . .175
19:38 . . . . . . . . . . .176
19:46 . . . . . . . . . . .177
19:47 . . . . . . . . . . .178
20:27 . . . . . . . . . . .55
20:38 . . . . . . . . . . .55
22:19-20 . . . . . . . . .70
22:28-30 . . . . . . . . .72
22:42 . . . . . . 189, 215
23:34 . . . . . . . . . . .74
23:43 . . . . . . . . . . .62

**John**
1:1. . . . . . . . . . . . .119
1:1, 14 . . . . . 117, 216
1:4. . . . . . . . . . . . .117
1:9. . . . . . . . . . . . .119
1:14. . . . . . . . . . . .185
1:17. . . . . . . . . . . . .6
1:23. . . . . . . . . . . .170
1:29. . . . . . . . . . . .185
2:12-23. . . . . . . . . .175
3:8. . . . . . . . . . . . .110
3:13. . . . . . . . . . . .63
3:17. . . . . . . . . . . .74
3:19-20. . . . . . .5, 220
5:24. . . . . . . . . . . .84

5:28-29. . . . . . . . . .56
5:30. . . . . . . . . . . .216
5:37-40. . . . . . . .84-85
6:1ff . . . . . . . . . . . .145
6:15. . . . . . . . . . . .170
6:32. . . . . . . . . . . .145
6:35. . . . . . . . . . . .123
7:24. . . . . . . . . . . .199
8:1-11. . . . . . . . . . .207
8:11. . . . . . . . . . . .207
8:12. . . . . . . . . . . .117
8:36. . . . . . . . . . . .203
10:3-4, 14 . . . . . . . .98
10:4-5. . . . . . . . . . .113
10:10-11 . . . . . . . .137
10:16 . . . . . . . . . . .99
10:30 . . . . . . . . . . .216
11:11 . . . . . . . . . . .56
12:32 . . . . . . . . . . .117
12:36 . . . . . . . . . . .117
12:46-48 . . . . . . . .213
13:13 . . . . . . . .83, 112
13:29 . . . . . . . . . . .145
14:6. . . . . . . . . . . .119
14:16-26 . . . . . .83-84
15:15-17 . . . . . . . .180
15:18-20 . . . . . . . .188
18:11 . . . . . . . . . . .169
20:23 . . . . . . . . . . .213
21:12ff . . . . . . . . . .181

**Acts**
1:8. . . . . . . . . . . . .187
2:17-21. . . . . . . . . .82
2:17-18. . . . . . . . . .105
2:34. . . . . . . . . . . .63
3:6. . . . . . . . . .88, 145
3:12-23. . . . . . . . . .89
4:30. . . . . . . . . . . .146
4:32-35. . . . . . . . . .146
5:1-11. . . . . . . . . . .146
5:36-37. . . . . . . . . .172
6:1-6. . . . . . . . . . . .121

7:60. . . . . . . . . . . .62
11:27-30 . . . . . . . .147
13:6. . . . . . . . . . . .112
13:36 . . . . . . . . . . .62
15:1. . . . . . . . . . . .114
15:5. . . . . . . . . . . .115
15:17 . . . . . . . . . . .115
15:22 . . . . . . . . . . .115
15:25 . . . . . . . . . . .115
15:28 . . . . . . . . . . .115
23:8. . . . . . . . . . . .55

**Romans**
1:17. . . . . . . 9, 76, 224
2:5-11. . . . . . . . . . .76
2:15-16. . . . . . . . . .75
2:16. . . . . . . . . . . .56
3:9-12. . . . . . . . . . .34
3:10. . . . . . . . . . . .77
3:21-25. . . . . . . . . .77
4:1-8. . . . . . . . . . . .9
4:22. . . . . . . . . . . .220
5:1. . . . . . . . . . . . .9
5:8-10. . . . . . . . . . .58
5:9-10. . . . . . . . . . .63
5:14. . . . . . . . . . . .78
5:15. . . . . . . . . . . .78
6:1. . . . . . . . . . . . .75
6:3-4. . . . . . . . . . . .215
6:4. . . . . . . . . . . . .78
6:10-13. . . . . . . .78-79
6:15. . . . . . . . . . . .75
6:17-18. . . . . . . . . .79
7:15. . . . . . . . . . . .65
8:2-10. . . . . . . . .79-80
8:14-17. . . . . . . . . .189
8:24. . . . . . . . . . . .64
8:31-38. . . . . . . . . .229
9:27. . . . . . . . . .60, 63
10:9. . . . . . 64, 77, 119
10:13 . . . . . . . . . . .64
11:14 . . . . . . . . . . .63
11:26 . . . . . . . . . . .63

12:2. . . . . . . . . . . . .183
12:14-21 . . . .181-182
15:26 . . . . . . . . . .147
16:25-26 . . . . . . . .75

**1 Corinthians**
1:17ff . . . . . . . . . .204
1:18. . . . . . . . .64, 116
1:21. . . . . . . . . . . .64
1:25. . . . . . . . . . . .178
1:30. . . . . . . . . . . .34
3:15. . . . . . . . . . . .63
5:1. . . . . . . . . . . . .204
5:2. . . . . . . . . . . . .204
5:3-5 . . . . . . . . . . .204
5:5. . . . . . . . . . .56, 63
6:5. . . . . . . . . . . . .113
6:9-10. . . . . . . . . . .76
6:19-20. . . . . . . . . .76
7:10. . . . . . . . . . . .112
7:16. . . . . . . . . . . .64
7:39. . . . . . . . . . . .62
9:22. . . . . . . . . . . .64
10:33 . . . . . . . . . . .64
11:5. . . . . . . . . . . .104
11:11-12 . . . . . . . .104
11:22 . . . . . . . . . . .103
11:24-25 . . . . . . . .70
11:25 . . . . . . . . . . .92
11:27 . . . . . . . . . . .103
11:30 . . . . . . . . . . .62
12:1-11. . . . . .109-110
12:3. . . . . . . . . . . .120
12:10 . . . . . . . . . . .113
12:27 . . . . . . . . . . .103
12:28 . . . . . . . . . . .110
12:31 . . . . . . . . . . .110
13:4. . . . . . . . . . . .109
14:1-5. . . . . . . . .82-83
14:18 . . . . . . . . . . .82
14:26-31 . . . .110-111
14:27 . . . . . . . . . . .120
14:32 . . . . . . . . . . .111

14:34 . . . . . . . . . . .120
14:35 . . . . . . . . . . .120
14:40 . . . . . . . . . . .104
15:2. . . . . . . . . . . .64
15:6-20. . . . . . . . . .62

**2 Corinthians**
1:21-22. . . . . . . . . .90
2:4-11. . . . . . . . . . .205
2:15. . . . . . . . . . . .64
3:6. . . . . . . . . . . . .92
4:4. . . . . . . . . . . . .183
5:18. . . . . . . . 117, 188
5:19. . . . . . . . . . . .217
5:21. . . . . . . . . . . .9
6:4-10. . . . . . .188-189
7:10. . . . . . . . . . . .232
8:8-9 . . . . . . . . . . .147
8:13-15. . . . . . . . . .147
10:3-5 . . . . . . . . . .182

**Galatians**
1:8f . . . . . . . . . . . .120
2:11. . . . . . . . . . . .102
3:26-29. . . . . . . . . .104
5:22-23. . . . . . . . . .90
6:14. . . . . . . . . . . .178

**Ephesians**
2:5, 8. . . . . . . . . . .64
2:11-22. . . . . . . . . .101
3:8-11. . . . . . . . . . .100
3:16-21. . . . . . . . . .12
4:32. . . . . . . . . . . .108
5:21. . . . . . . . . . . .108
6:12-17. . . . . .183-184

**Philippians**
2:6-10. . . . . . .74, 217
3:9. . . . . . . . . . . . .9
3:10-11. . . . . . . . . .189

**Colossians**
1:13. . . . . . . . . . . .204
1:19-20. . . . . . . . . .217
1:24. . . . . . . . . . . .189
1:27. . . . . . . . . . . .80
2:13-16. . . . . . . . . .102
3:5-6 . . . . . . . . . . .140

**1 Thessalonians**
2:16. . . . . . . . . . . .64
4:13-15. . . . . . . . . .62
4:15. . . . . . . . . . . .112
4:16. . . . . . . . . . . .63
5:1-5 . . . . . . . . . . .56
5:9. . . . . . . . . . . . .58

**2 Thessalonians**
1:6-10. . . . . . . . . . .56
2:1-3 . . . . . . . . . . .56
2:10. . . . . . . . . . . .63
2:13. . . . . . . . . . . .90

**1 Timothy**
1:15. . . . . . . . . . . .63
2:4. . . . . . . . . . . . .63
2:15. . . . . . . . . . . .64
4:16. . . . . . . . . . . .64
6:9-10. . . . . . . . . . .140

**2 Timothy**
1:9. . . . . . . . . . . . .64
4:18. . . . . . . . . .58, 63

**Titus**
2:13. . . . . . . . . . . .216
3:5. . . . . . . . . . . . .64

**Philemon**
6 . . . . . . . . . . . . . .103
15-16 . . . . . . . . . . .102

**Hebrews**
1:3. . . . . . . . . . . . .216

2:10-18..........186
3:12-15..........226
4:12-13..........220
8:12...............60
9:11-15...........70
10:24-25 ......96-97
10:26-27 .........56
11 ...............97
12:2...............4
12:22-25 .........97

James
1:21..............85
2:1-6............103
2:21-24..........224

1 Peter
2:9-10...........97
4:18..............60

2 Peter
2:1.............113
2:7-10...........56
3:4..............62
3:10-17........58-59

1 John
1:8-10..........210
2:3-7...........120
2:27.............81
4:1.............113
4:1ff ..........120
4:2.............120
4:7-21..........184
4:8-16........95, 230
4:17..........56-57

Revelation
2:7..............14
3:20.............112
4:2-11..........118
5:9-12..........186
7:9-17..........212

12:10-11 .......187
15:8............186
17:5............148
17:5-6..........155
17:14 ...... 184, 186
18:1-24.....148-149
18:4-5..........150
19:1-9......150-151
19:8............196
19:10 ..........120
19:11-21 .......185
19:15 ..........200
19:20ff .........218
20:14-15 .........31
21:1.............31
21:3-6........29, 86
21:23-24 .........28
21:23-27 .....28, 117
21:25-27 .....31, 211
22:1-2...........28
22:2.............29
22:3..........24, 57
22:13 ..........216

Apocrypha and
Pseudepigrapha

2 Maccabees
7:9..............54
12:43-44 .........54

1 Enoch
50:1; 51:1-5.......55
50:2-5...........57
69:27-29 .........91

Jubilees
17:15-18:12......233
33:13 ..........208

Odes of Solomon
11 ............14-15